Your World

Editor: Katie Puckett
Designer: John Jamieson
Managing Editor: Miranda Smith

Activity illustrations: Gina Suter
Additional design: Joanne Brown
DTP coordinator: Nicky Studdart
Production controller: Kelly Johnson
Artwork archivists: Wendy Allison, Steve Robinson
Indexer: Sue Lightfoot

KINGFISHER
Larousse Kingfisher Chambers Inc.
95 Madison Avenue
New York, New York 10016

First published in 1999
2 4 6 8 10 9 7 5 3

3(1SBF)/0500/SF/HBM/128IMA

Wilkes, Angela.
Your world / by Angela Wilkes. —1st ed.
p.   cm.
Includes index.
Summary: Presents information for young children on a wide variety
of topics, arranged in such categories as The Universe, The World
Around You, Prehistoric Life, Plant Life, Reptiles and Amphibians,
Birds and Mammals, Your Body, People and Places, Transport,
and How Things Work.
ISBN 0-7534-5217-0
1. Science Miscellanea Juvenile literature.   [1. Science
Miscellanea.] I. Title.
Q173.W68   1999
500—dc21   99-28572
CIP

Printed in China

Your World

KING*f*ISHER

NEW YORK

Contents

Birds and Mammals

All kinds of animals from around the world. Find out how to hunt like a tiger, fly like a bird, or hop like a kangaroo.

Your Body

Learn how all the parts of your body work to keep you healthy. Find out what happens when you eat, jump, or sleep.

People and Places

Find out about the work, homes, customs, and festivals of people in different countries.

Trains, Boats, and Planes

Different ways to travel, from bicycles to race cars, trucks to trains, submarines to jumbo jets.

How Things Work

An introduction to the science of everyday life. Why things float, how things move, shadows, sounds, and seesaws.

Index and acknowledgments

About this book

*Y*our *World* is full of information about the world in which we live. You can find out all about animals and plants, people and places, transportation, outer space, and how things work.

Some pages have a special activity box. There are lots of things to make, games to play, and experiments to try. Ask an adult to help you with activities that use paint. Enjoy your book!

Angela Willkes

ACTIVITY BOX

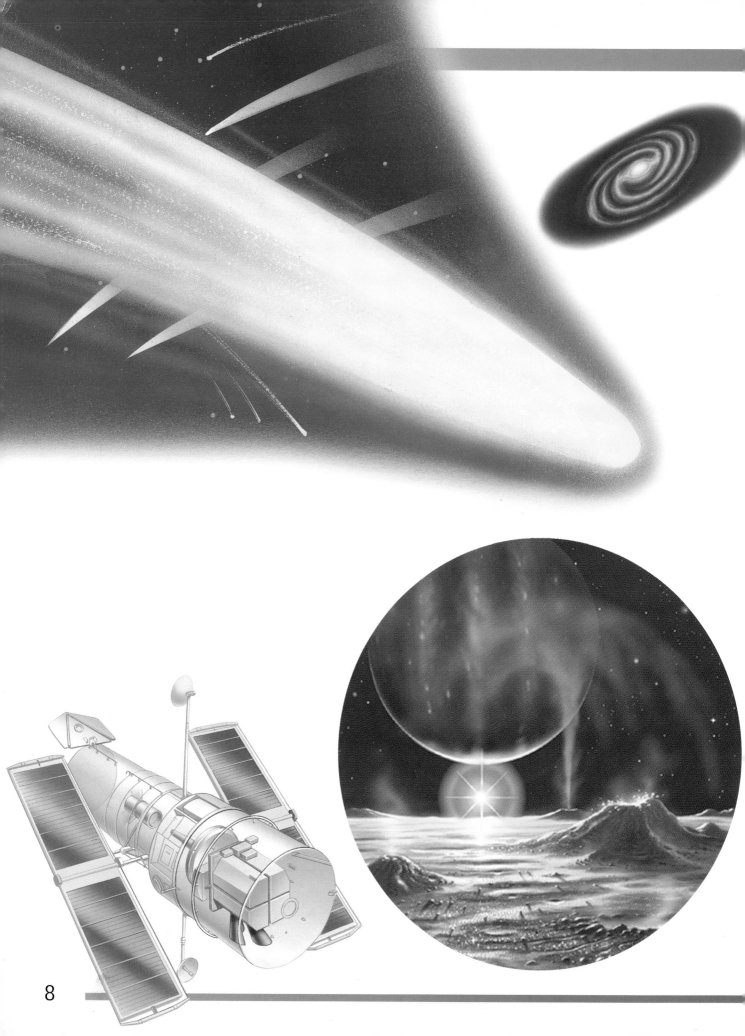

The Universe

The Universe

Everything that exists is part of the Universe. The Earth is in the Universe, and so are the Sun, the Moon, and everything else out in space. The Universe is enormous. No one knows how big it is, or where it begins and ends.

Some red giants grow into huge supergiants.

The Universe is made up of billions of stars. Stars are huge balls of burning gases. New stars are born all the time from clouds of dust and gas. Old stars fade and grow cold.

A star shines for billions of years.

Then it swells up into a big star called a red giant.

The outer layers of the star may escape into space.

A small, spinning part of the star may remain after a supernova. It is called a pulsar. It sends out beams of light.

When a giant star dies, there is a huge explosion called a supernova.

Sometimes a black hole is left after a supernova. It can suck in anything that is nearby.

All that is left of the star is its dead core. This is called a white dwarf. It slowly cools down and grows dim.

Millions of years later, the star is just a cold black globe.

Night sky

On a clear night you can see that the sky is full of stars. Many of them form patterns in the sky called constellations. Long ago, people gave constellations names to make it easier to recognize them.

Astronomers use telescopes to look more closely at the stars and to see farther into space.

People in the northern part of the world see the stars shown here in the sky at night.

This constellation is named Pegasus, after a mythical horse.

The Hubble space telescope orbits the Earth. It can see much farther into space than the largest telescopes on the ground.

People who live in the southern part of the world see a different set of stars. There are some very bright stars here.

This group of stars is known as the Southern Cross.

Galaxies

The Universe is made of gigantic groups of stars, called galaxies. There are billions of stars in each galaxy. Our planet Earth and the Sun are near the edge of a galaxy called the Milky Way.

If you look at the sky on a clear night, you may see a faint band of stars. This is part of the Milky Way. Our galaxy is a giant spiral of stars, slowly moving around a large group of stars in the middle.

The central part of a galaxy is called the nucleus

GALAXY PICTURE

Draw a spiral galaxy with glue on a big piece of black construction paper. Sprinkle glitter over the glue. Tilt the paper up to shake off any loose glitter.

New stars form from areas of gas and dust

Galaxies are different shapes and sizes. These are the three main types.

Irregular-shaped galaxy

Egg-shaped galaxy

Spiral galaxy

The Solar System

A family of planets, moons, comets, and other chunks of rock is constantly spinning around the Sun. This family is called the Solar System. There are nine planets in the Solar System. They are made of rock, liquid, metal, or gas.

The planets in the Solar System are millions of miles apart. They are very different from each other. Mercury is the closest planet to the Sun and Pluto is the farthest away. Jupiter is the largest planet. It is so big that all the other planets could fit inside it together.

Jupiter

Mercury

Venus

Earth

Mars

Orbit

The Sun, the planets, and their moons all spin like tops. At the same time, they travel around the Sun. The paths they follow are called orbits.

PLANETARIUM

Draw the Sun and planets on construction paper. Color and cut them out. Ask an adult to help you hang them from the ceiling in the right order of their distance from the Sun.

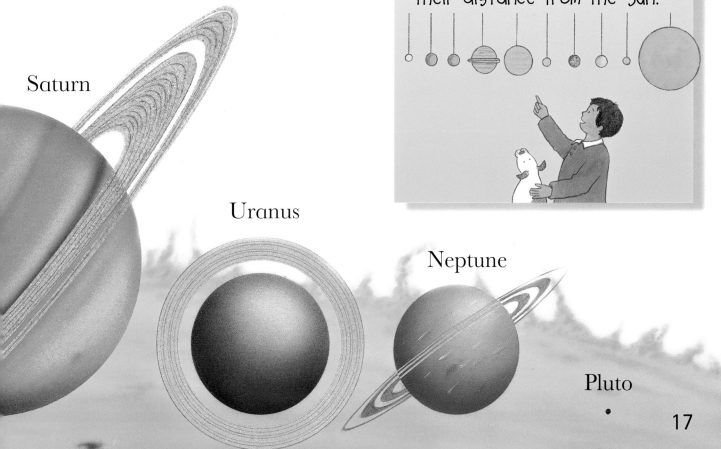

Saturn

Uranus

Neptune

Pluto

The Sun

The Sun is a star, just like the other stars you see in the sky at night. It is an enormous ball of burning gases, millions of times bigger than the Earth. The Sun gives off heat and light. Without it, the Earth would be cold, dark, and lifeless.

The Sun's rays can damage your skin if you spend too long outside on a sunny day. People use special creams to protect their skin.

Sun

Earth

The Earth is the third planet from the Sun. It travels around it at a distance of about 93 million miles. The Earth moves very fast, but it still takes a year (365 days) for it to complete its orbit.

The Sun is made mainly of a gas called hydrogen. The hottest part of the Sun is its core. Hot gases bubble up to the surface. They form a halo of gases called the corona. The dark patches on the surface of the Sun are sunspots. They are less hot than the rest of its surface.

Flaming jets of gas can flare up from the surface of the Sun.

Secondary layer

Core

Corona

Sunspots

Close to the Sun

Mercury and Venus are the two planets in the Solar System closest to the Sun. They are both much, much hotter than the Earth. There are no signs of water on either planet. Nothing can grow or live on them.

Mercury spins very slowly, but it races around the Sun. It is burning hot on the side facing the Sun and icy cold on the other side.

Mercury is bare and rocky. On the surface it looks a lot like our Moon. It is covered with hills and giant hollows called craters.

Venus is about the same size as the Earth. It is the hottest planet of all. Its surface is covered by thick clouds of poisonous gases. These trap heat from the Sun.

You can often see Venus shining brightly in the sky just after sunset or before sunrise. It always looks as if it is very close to the Sun.

The surface of Venus is almost all flat, but there are a lot of old volcanoes, and raised areas of the lava that has flowed from them. Scientists think some of the volcanoes may still erupt from time to time.

The Earth

The Earth is the planet on which we live. It is a huge ball of rock spinning in space. The Earth is the only planet with water on it, and air for plants and animals to breathe. This is why there is life on Earth, but not on any other planet.

This is what the Earth looks like from space. Most of its surface is covered with water. The brown and green areas are land. The white patterns are clouds swirling in the sky.

It takes the Earth a day (24 hours) to spin once. It is day on the side of the Earth that faces the Sun. It is night on the side that faces away from it.

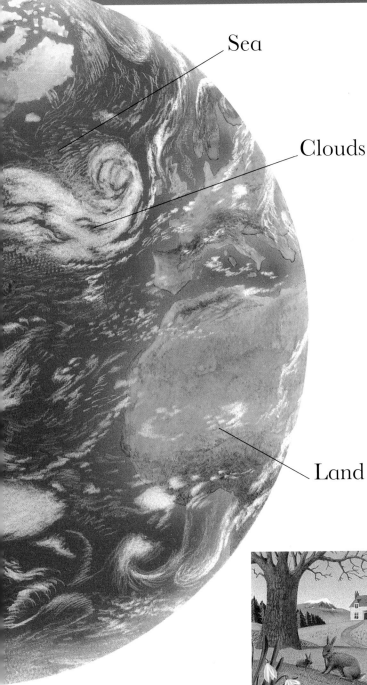

Sea

Clouds

Land

NIGHT AND DAY

Hold a globe and ask a friend to shine a flashlight at it. Make the globe spin. The flashlight is like the Sun. It is day in the area lit by the flashlight and night everywhere else.

Spring

Fall

The Earth spins at an angle, so the seasons change as the Earth moves around the Sun. It is summer in the part of the world that is closest to the Sun.

Summer

Winter

The Moon

The Moon is the closest object in space to us. It is a little over one-fourth the size of the Earth, and takes about a month to travel around it. The Moon has no air or water, so nothing can grow on it or live there.

The Moon turns as it orbits the Earth, so that the same side of it is always facing the Earth. The dark areas on the Moon are plains.

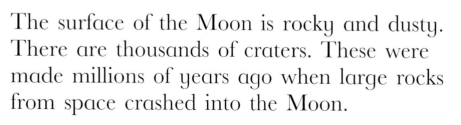

The surface of the Moon is rocky and dusty. There are thousands of craters. These were made millions of years ago when large rocks from space crashed into the Moon.

New moon

Half moon,
first quarter

Full moon

Half moon,
last quarter

Crescent
waning

The Moon looks as if it changes shape. This is because we only see the part of it that is lit by the Sun. The sunlit part changes as the Moon moves around the Earth. Every month the Moon waxes (seems to grow bigger), then wanes (grows smaller).

MOON DIARY

Make a chart with a square for each day of the month. Draw what the moon looks like and describe it every night for a month.

Mars

Mars is the fourth planet from the Sun. It is the planet most like the Earth, but it is much colder because it is farther from the Sun. A day on Mars is about the same length as a day on Earth. Mars also has summer and winter seasons.

Mars is often called the Red Planet because its rocks are a rusty red color. Winds and storms blow reddish dust around, making Mars look pink from Earth.

Deimos

Phobos

Mars is circled by two small, dark moons, called Phobos and Deimos. They are strangely shaped, a bit like lumpy potatoes.

Between Mars and Jupiter, millions of small lumps of rock circle the Sun. These miniplanets are called asteroids. Most of them only measure a few miles across.

Fragments of rock

Larger rock

Mars is covered with old volcanoes and rocky canyons. Scientists think that there may have been rivers there in the past.

The giant planets

Beyond the asteroids are two enormous gas planets, Jupiter and Saturn. Both of them are circled by rings and moons. Jupiter is the largest planet in the Solar System, larger than all the others put together.

Icy cold clouds cover the surface of Jupiter. Strong winds blow these into bands of different colors.

Swirling clouds

Jupiter has 16 moons. One of them, Io, has active volcanoes on it. Io's rocky surface (left) is dyed red and orange by sulfur from its volcanoes.

Saturn is a spinning ball of gas and liquid. It is circled by 18 rocky moons. The planet's surface is covered in fast-moving clouds.

Icy rings

Strong winds race around Saturn

Saturn's rings are really thousands of narrow ringlets. They are made of millions of pieces of glittering ice. Most of these are small, but some measure several miles across.

MAKE JUPITER

Have an adult mix turpentine with drops of yellow and red oil paint. Put drops of color in a tray of water and swirl it around with a paintbrush. Lay a circle of paper on top. Lift it off and hang it up to dry.

Distant planets

Out near the edge of the Solar System there are three planets: Uranus, Neptune, and Pluto. They are so far away that they can't be seen with the naked eye. No space probe has visited Pluto, the most distant planet, so we do not know much about it.

Neptune is a bluish color. It has eight moons. Triton, its largest moon, is the coldest object in the Solar System. Its cracked, frozen surface is dotted with volcanoes. These erupt with plumes of black dust and gases.

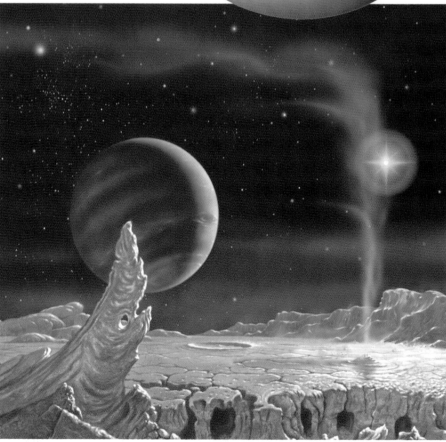

Pluto is the smallest planet of all. It has one moon, called Charon, which is half its size. Pluto follows an oval-shaped orbit around the Sun. This means that it is sometimes closer to the Sun than Neptune.

Uranus is four times bigger than the Earth. It is the only planet that spins on its side. It is circled by 15 moons and about 11 narrow rings of small rocks.

Moving stars

You can see many things in the sky that are not stars or planets. Meteors and comets are burning lumps of rock that look like streaks of light whizzing across the sky.

Meteors are often called shooting stars. They are actually flecks of space dust which burn up in the air surrounding the Earth.

Lumps of space rock that crash into Earth are called meteorites. Even small ones like this make massive craters (left).

A comet hangs in the sky like a huge star with a tail. Comets are lumps of ice and rock that orbit the Sun. Their tails can be many millions of miles long.

Crumbling pieces of rock and ice

Nucleus

Jets of dust and gas

The Sun's heat melts the surface of the comet, making a cloud of gas and dust that blows into a giant tail.

Space discovery

One of the ways we find out more about the Universe is by sending spacecraft into space. Fast rockets take satellites, probes, and astronauts to study the planets and moons. These then send information back to scientists on Earth.

Rockets are the only machines powerful enough to escape the Earth's pull and travel into space. A rocket is made up of parts called stages. Each one has its own engine and fuel, and it drops off once its fuel runs out.

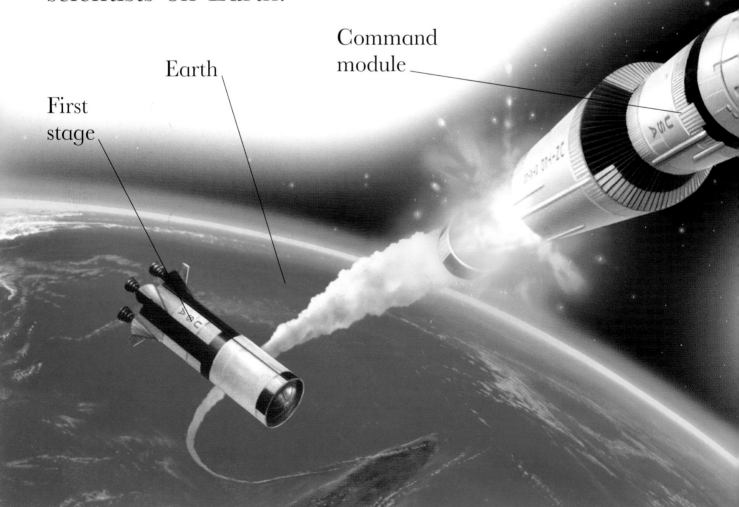

First stage

Earth

Command module

Space probes, such as Mariner 10, are unmanned spacecraft that explore the Solar System. Mariner 10 flew past Mercury three times and took thousands of photographs of its surface.

Spacecraft

Different sized rockets are used to launch things into space. Ariane launches satellites and probes. The shuttle is launched by two rockets. Saturn V carried astronauts to the moon.

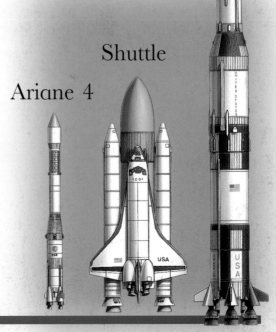

Saturn V

Shuttle

Ariane 4

Astronauts

Human beings can't normally live in space. There is no air to breathe and everything is weightless. If astronauts are going to spend time in space, they must have air to breathe and the right living conditions.

Solar panels make electric power

Mir space station

Mir is a Russian space station that orbits the Earth. Astronauts travel there in spacecraft that dock with Mir. Supplies are sent out to them in unmanned spacecraft.

Scientists work in this area

Astronauts float in space

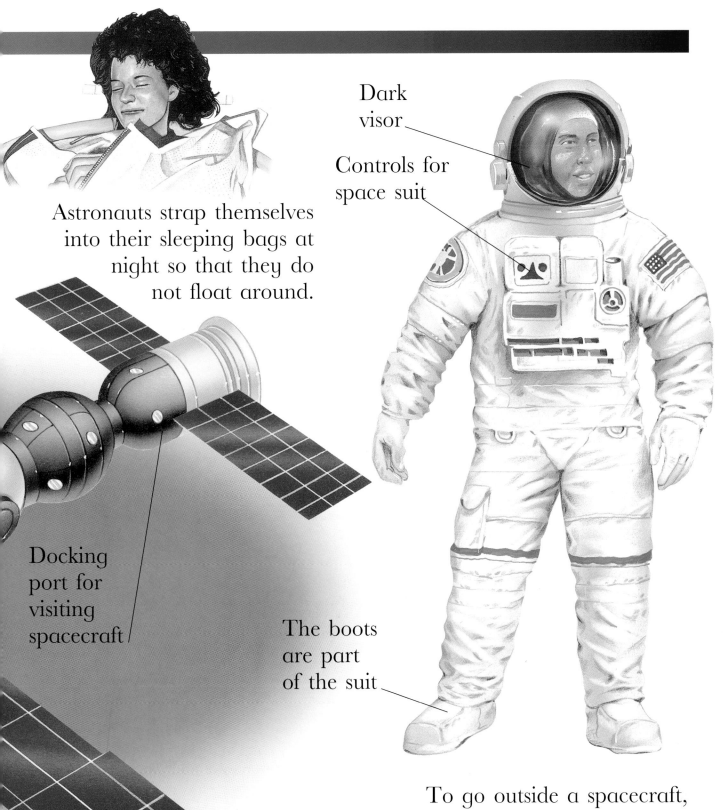

Astronauts strap themselves into their sleeping bags at night so that they do not float around.

Dark visor

Controls for space suit

Docking port for visiting spacecraft

The boots are part of the suit

To go outside a spacecraft, an astronaut has to wear a thick space suit. It protects him and keeps him at the right temperature. The astronaut carries all the air and water he needs in his backpack.

Space shuttle

Fuel tank

The space shuttle takes off like a rocket, but when it comes back to Earth, it lands like a glider. Shuttles can be used over and over again.

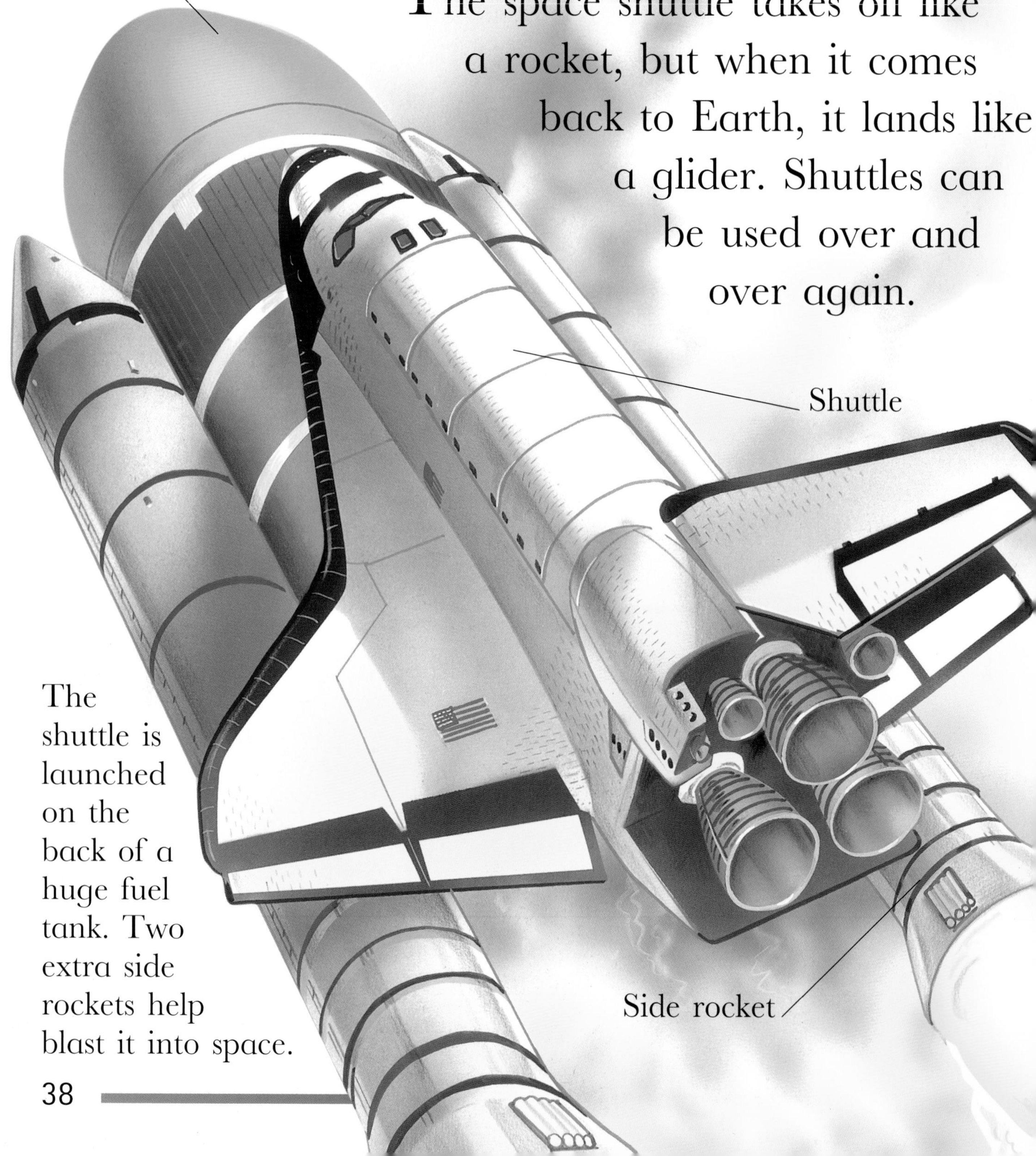

Shuttle

The shuttle is launched on the back of a huge fuel tank. Two extra side rockets help blast it into space.

Side rocket

38

Special tiles cover the shuttle to keep it from burning up as it speeds back to Earth.

Side rocket

After blastoff, the two side rockets drop back to Earth on huge parachutes.

ROCKET!

Thread a long piece of string through a straw. Tie the string to two chairs. Blow up a balloon and seal it with a binder clip. Tape the balloon to the straw. Open the clip and watch your rocket shoot forward.

The World Around Us

About our world

The Earth is amazingly varied. It has hot deserts, huge oceans, steamy rain forests, and frozen lands. Each part of the Earth has its own climate, or type of weather. The plants and animals adapt to where they live.

The landscape changes wherever you go. There are natural features, such as mountains. Landmarks such as oil wells have been made by people.

4

6

5

1

3

2

Most of our planet is covered by water. A thin blanket of air surrounds the Earth. Weather is produced by changes in this blanket of air.

1. Sea
2. River
3. Lake
4. Rain
5. Waterfall
6. Mountain
7. Forest
8. Oil well
9. Animals
10. City

Volcano

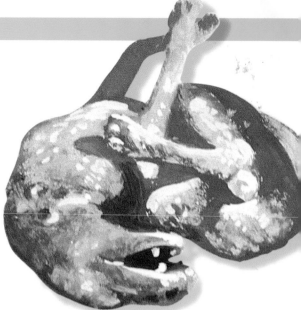

A volcano is a mountain that explodes. Deep below the surface of the Earth, the rocks are so hot that they melt. When a volcano erupts, this red-hot melted rock bursts out of a hole at the top of the mountain.

This dog was buried in the lava from a volcano in Pompeii, Italy, in A.D. 79.

ERUPTION!

Make a construction paper cone, leaving a hole at the top. Put a shallow plastic bowl in the hole. Ask an adult to add a little red powder paint and some baking soda. Carefully add some vinegar and watch the volcano erupt!

Hot, melted rock is called magma when it is under the ground, and lava when it reaches the surface.

During an eruption, boiling lava pours down the mountainsides, destroying everything in its path. The lava cools slowly in the air. Later, it hardens into new rock.

Earthquakes

The top layer of the Earth, the crust, is like a giant jigsaw puzzle. It is made up of huge, interlocking pieces that shift very slowly all the time. Sometimes they don't move smoothly and this makes the ground shake. It is an earthquake!

An earthquake is very frightening. The ground trembles and buildings can collapse, killing people. Earthquakes usually last only a few minutes but they can cause a lot of damage.

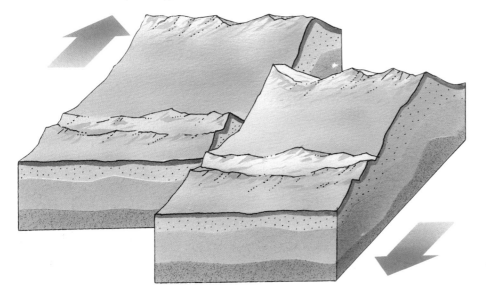

An earthquake happens when two pieces of the Earth's crust, or plates, try to move past each other and scrape together. They push and grind in opposite directions, making the rocks tilt and slip.

The shock waves from an earthquake can create giant waves called "tsunamis," which speed across the sea. They tower up when they reach land, destroying whole villages and towns.

Earthquakes may cause fires because underground fuel lines are broken.

Cracks large enough to swallow cars can open up in the ground.

47

Shaping the land

The landscape is changing slowly all the time. It is worn away by water and wind. The sea makes cliffs, and rivers carve out valleys. Even the hardest rocks are worn down.

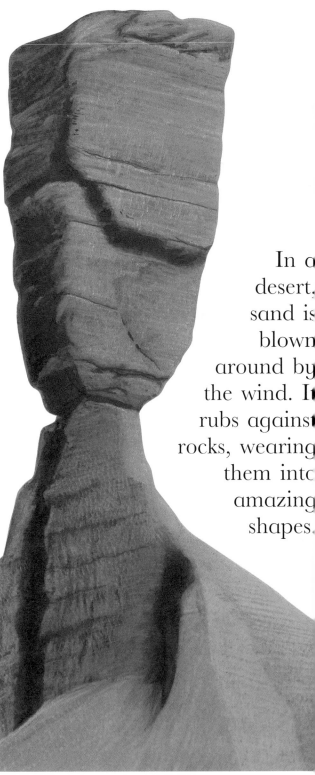

In a desert, sand is blown around by the wind. It rubs against rocks, wearing them into amazing shapes.

Water trickling through limestone creates underground caves with huge stalactites and stalagmites.

The Grand Canyon is a giant gorge in Arizona. It has been carved out of the rocks over thousands of years by the Colorado River. As the river has worked its way downward, it has exposed different layers of rock. The lower down the canyon the layer of rock, the older it is.

Weather

The weather changes from day to day, and from season to season. It may be sunny one day and rainy the next. If the sun comes out when it is raining, you might see a rainbow. Weather is different all over the world. Some places are always hot while others are freezing cold.

Flashes of lightning are giant sparks of electricity that jump between storm clouds and the ground. Thunder is the noise made by the lightning.

The colors in a rainbow are always in the same order— red, orange, yellow, green, blue, indigo, and violet.

Clouds are made of millions of tiny drops of water. Some are a sign of fine weather. Others bring rain and thunderstorms.

Cirrus

Stratus

Cumulonimbus

Cumulus

WEATHER CHART

Draw a grid on a large piece of paper and write the days of the week at the top. Look at the weather every day and put the correct weather symbol on your chart.

Sunny   Cloudy   Rainy   Windy

Some places have violent storms called tornadoes. A tornado looks like a dark funnel of cloud. In fact, it is a whirlwind that spins along the ground and can cause a lot of damage. Fast winds whirl around a central spot where there is hardly any wind at all.

Water cycle

The air is full of water vapor—tiny drops of water too small to see. Rain doesn't just come from the sky, but from the water that is all around us. The amount of water on Earth stays the same, but it keeps moving around.

The clouds grow heavier and are blown over the land.

Water vapor rises and forms clouds.

Water from the sea turns to water vapor.

As water is warmed by the Sun, it seems to dry up. In fact, it rises into the air as water vapor. As water vapor rises, it cools down and turns back into drops of water. These form clouds, and it rains.

If it is cold, it may snow rather than rain. The drops of water in the clouds freeze into ice crystals and these join together to make delicate snowflakes. No two snowflakes are ever the same.

Water in the clouds falls as rain, hail, sleet, or snow.

Rainwater runs into rivers and flows back into the sea.

MAKE A SNOW GLOBE

Find a jar with a tight lid. Glue small plastic toys inside the lid. Pour water into the jar until it is nearly full. Add some glitter and screw on the lid. Shake the jar and turn it upside down.

Life of a river

Many rivers start life in the mountains. Streams of rainwater run from high to low land. They join together and grow into a river that flows downhill toward the sea.

A river provides food for all kinds of creatures There are many fish, such as this salmon.

Rain falls high in the mountains.

Streams run into each other.

Waterfall

A river changes at each stage of its journey. It starts life as a bubbling stream, but by the time it reaches the sea, it is wider and flows much more slowly.

The river grows wider

Reeds and rushes grow along a river.

When a river drops sharply downhill over steep ledges of rock, it makes waterfalls. These splash and make a lot of spray.

The river winds its way across the land

All rivers end in the sea. The place where a river flows into the sea is the mouth of the river.

Marshes

Marshes and swamps are wet, boggy areas of land next to rivers or the sea. Some of them look like lakes dotted with islands. Others look more like grasslands because so many reeds grow there.

1. Mangrove roots
2. Raccoon
3. Terrapin
4. Roseate spoonbill
5. Alligator
6. Tarpon
7. Zebra butterfly
8. Woodpecker
9. Rough green snake
10. Green tree frog

Marshes are home to many exotic birds and animals. The tree roots and reeds make good homes, and there are a lot of fish to eat in the water.

DRAGONFLY

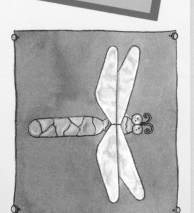

Pattern

Copy the dragonfly pattern onto a large piece of paper. Glue foil gum wrappers on the body and wings. Use buttons for the eyes and pipe cleaners for the antennae.

9

7

8

5

10

6

Woodlands

Woods grow in parts of the world where it is never very hot or very cold. They are green and shady in summer, but the trees lose their leaves in winter and the wood looks bare. Woods provide food and homes for many different animals.

Birds and squirrels take shelter high in the trees. Badgers and foxes dig burrows beneath the tree roots. Deer and boars hide among the bushes and shrubs.

1. Fox
2. Jay
3. Wild boar
4. Porcupine
5. Sparrow hawk
6. Gray squirrel
7. Red deer
8. Speckled wood butterfly
9. Badger
10. Great spotted woodpecker

Rain forest

Steamy rain forests grow in hot countries where it rains nearly every day. It is hot all year round, so there is no summer or winter. More plants and animals live in rain forests than anywhere else in the world.

Colorful parrots roost in the treetops.

The trees grow huge in a rain forest because it rains so much. It is dark and shady down on the ground, but bright and sunny in the treetops. There, high above the ground, the branches lace together to form a canopy where flowers and fruit grow.

Bushbabies and other small animals come out at night to hunt for food.

The largest hunters in a rain forest are big cats such as this tiger.

Look for all these things in the big picture.

1. Creeper
2. Gibbon
3. Arrow poison frog
4. Toadstools
5. Macaw
6. Butterflies
7. Leafcutter ants
8. Toucan

63

Grasslands

Around the world there are huge grasslands that stretch for thousands of miles. After it rains, the grass is green, but for most of the year it is dry and brown. It does not rain often enough for many trees to grow here.

The savannas in Africa are enormous grassy plains dotted with a few thorny bushes and trees. Many wild animals live here. They move around to find water and the freshest green grass.

The North American grasslands are called prairies. There, prairie dogs burrow under the ground to make their homes. One of them always guards the entrance.

1. Gazelles
2. Giraffes
3. Zebra
4. Elephant
5. Lioness and cub
6. Eland

Deserts

Deserts are the driest places on Earth. Sometimes it doesn't rain for years. Most deserts are burning hot in the day and freezing cold at night. Some are cold all the time. Yet they are still home to some unusual plants and animals.

1. Elf owl
2. Gila woodpecker
3. Saguaro cactus
4. Bearded lizard

Camels can live for days without food or water. They have flat feet for walking on sand and long eyelashes to keep sand out of their eyes.

The American deserts are bare and rocky. Spiky plants called cacti grow there. They store water in their fat stems.

Some deserts are sandy. Strong winds blow the sand into hills called dunes. The only places where plants and trees grow is near water holes, called oases.

5. Rattlesnake
6. Roadrunner
7. Kangaroo rat
8. Kit fox

SAND PICTURE

Draw a picture of the desert on construction paper with a glue stick. Pour sand over the glue. Shake the loose sand off to see your picture.

3

2

4

6

8

5

7

Cold lands

The North and South poles are at the top and bottom of the Earth. The land and sea around them are frozen. They are covered with snow and ice all year round.

Reindeer live in the Arctic, the area around the North Pole. They dig through the snow to eat plants called lichens. They move south in the winter to find more food.

Penguins bring their chicks up on the frozen seas near the South Pole.

The arctic hare's fur turns white in winter.

The polar bear is the biggest hunter in the Arctic. Its thick, oily coat keeps it warm. Polar bears are good swimmers. They hunt for seals under the ice, or wait for them by the blowholes where they come up for air.

Saving our planet

Our planet faces many problems. The air and seas are getting polluted, or dirty, and some plants and animals are dying out. The Earth's natural fuels, such as gas, coal, and oil, are being used up.

Fumes from factories and cars pollute the air with chemicals. These dissolve in clouds and make acid rain, which harms wildlife and plants.

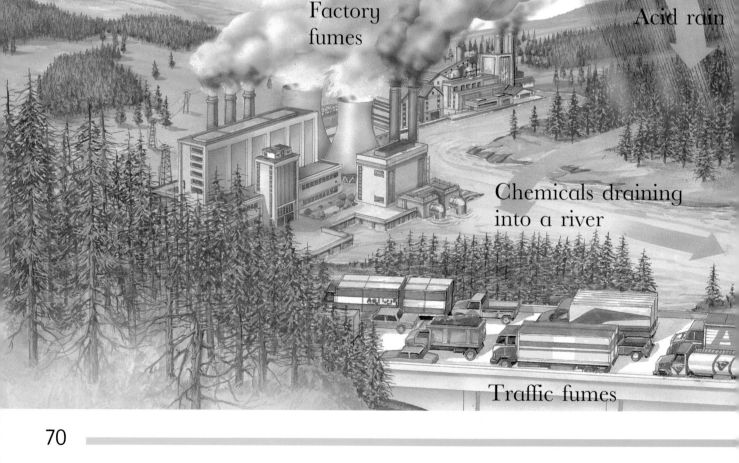

Factory fumes

Acid rain

Chemicals draining into a river

Traffic fumes

Scientists are inventing new forms of energy that don't cause pollution. They can use energy from the sun or wind to make electricity.

Solar-powered electric car

RECYCLE IT!

Sort your family's garbage into boxes for paper, glass, and aluminum cans. Take them to your local recycling center.

Animals are hunted and their homes are destroyed or polluted. The humpback whale (below) has been hunted so much that it may become extinct.

Humpback whale

Prehistoric Life

Clues to the past

Scientists find out about the history of the Earth by studying rocks. The remains of plants and animals that lived long ago have turned to stone and become fossils. They give us clues about what lived on Earth millions of years ago.

Plant-eating Triceratops

No one has ever seen a dinosaur. Scientists figure out what they looked like by putting together the fossils they find. Fossils take thousands of years to form. They are usually the hard parts of the body, such as bones and teeth.

Flat tooth of a plant-eating dinosaur

Meat-eating Tyrannosaurus Rex

Sharp teeth of a meat-eater

Fossil fern

Horsetails

Ferns

The fossil print on the rock above was made by a fern hundreds of millions of years ago. It looks like the ferns that are around now. Scientists have also found horsetail fossils, another plant that still exists today.

MAKE A FOSSIL

Shape some modeling clay into a square. Press a leaf into it to make a fossil print. Peel the leaf off, then bury the modeling clay "fossil" in a tray of dry sand. Brush off the sand to reveal the fossil.

Millions of years ago, shellfish called ammonites lived in the sea. When they died, they were buried in mud and sand. As more layers of mud built up, the ammonites slowly turned to rock, becoming fossils.

Ammonite fossil

Evolution

The Earth is millions of years old and is changing slowly all the time. As the Earth changes, so do the plants and animals that live here. They adapt according to where they live. The way that living things change is called evolution.

The first tiny fish lived in the sea about 500 million years ago.

About 395 million years ago, some animals moved onto the land. These were the amphibians.

Most of the animals that live on Earth today didn't exist in the past. Most of the animals that lived in the past no longer exist today. The first plants and animals were tiny and lived in the sea. Nowadays, there are all sorts of living things on every part of the planet.

Some animals become extinct, or die out, if their homes and lives are disturbed. The dodo was a large flightless bird that lived on the island of Mauritius. It was hunted by the people who first moved to the island and is now extinct.

Dinosaurs and other reptiles lived from 240 million years ago to 64 million years ago.

After the dinosaurs died out, mammals took over. The first ones were small, but later ones were larger.

The first humans lived about two million years ago. They may have evolved from apelike creatures.

First life

The first plants and animals lived in the sea. They were probably too small to see. The first animals had soft bodies, like jellyfish and worms. Soon there were animals with hard shells. The first fish appeared after this.

Many different sea creatures lived around a coral reef about 450 million years ago. They swam or crept along the seabed in search of things to eat.

1. Trilobite
2. Brachiopods
3. Graptolite

Fish were the first animals with bones. Duncleosteus was a monster fish. It was a fierce hunter with huge, sharp teeth.

AMMONITE ART

Draw an ammonite on white paper with a white crayon, copying the picture below. Paint all of the paper with watered-down blue-green paint. Your picture of the ammonite will appear where the waxy crayon lines are.

Dinosaur world

Dinosaurs appeared on our planet 228 million years ago. Some of them were enormous—the biggest animals to ever live on land. Others weren't much bigger than a chicken. They all died out about 64 million years ago.

All dinosaurs had scaly skins and laid eggs, like reptiles today. Some ate plants, while others were hunters. They lived alongside other reptiles and early kinds of birds and insects.

Many dinosaurs
lived near swamps.

1. Stegosaurus
2. Apatosaurus
3. Deinosuchus
4. Allosaurus
5. Archaeopteryx

Plant-eaters

The biggest dinosaurs of all were plant-eaters. They had barrel-shaped bodies and very long necks and tails. They lived in herds and moved around looking for food. They plucked leaves from high in the trees, as giraffes do today.

The weather was warm and wet at the time of the dinosaurs. There were forests of giant ferns and evergreens. Plant-eaters ate leaves, roots, and pinecones. They had peglike teeth for snipping leaves off trees.

1. Brachiosaurus
2. Apatosaurus
3. Diplodocus

Some plant-eaters looked
very strange. One was
called Parasaurolophus.
These dinosaurs had
mouths like beaks
and bony crests
on their heads. They could
blow out through these, and
may have tooted like
trombones.

2

3

DINOSAUR INVITE

Draw and color
a long-necked
dinosaur on a
wide piece of
construction paper. Fill in
your party details on the
back. Fold the paper as shown
into an accordion.

Meat-eaters

Some dinosaurs ate animals, and often other dinosaurs. Most meat-eaters were fierce and could move fast to catch their prey. Some of them hunted alone. Others hunted in packs.

Tyrannosaurus Rex was the biggest meat-eater of all. It had massive jaws and razor-sharp teeth for slicing through flesh.

Many meat-eaters had huge hooked claws for slashing out at the animals they chased.

Meat-eating dinosaurs didn't need to eat every day. One kill would provide enough food for several days. Some dinosaurs didn't hunt at all. Instead, they were scavengers, eating any dead or dying animals they found.

Asrovenator

Into battle

Plant-eating dinosaurs couldn't move very fast, so they had to defend themselves against hungry meat-eaters. Some plant-eaters grouped together for safety. Others had fierce horns to scare off enemies, and thick skin like armor.

Deinonychus was a small, fast meat-eater. Its name means "terrible claw" and refers to the long, curved claws on its back feet. Deinonychus was too small to kill a large plant-eater on its own, so it hunted in packs. The pack would attack together, wounding their victim with their claws and teeth.

Triceratops was armed with horns on its nose and above its eyes. It also had a huge bony neck shield and thick, leathery skin to help protect itself from enemies.

This armored dinosaur was called Euoplocephalus. It had bony plates and spikes along its back and a huge club at the end of its tail.

A TRICERATOPS MASK

Draw a Triceratops face like this on construction paper.
Make a nose horn out of paper and attach it to the mask with a paper fastener.
Tie a piece of thin elastic through holes at the sides of the mask.

Hatching out

Dinosaur babies hatched from eggs, just like reptiles do today. Some dinosaur mothers, including Maiasaura, made big nests on the ground in which they laid about 20 eggs. In 1984, a group of more than 20 Maiasaura nests was found on Egg Mountain in Montana.

Dinosaur eggs

Fossils of dinosaur eggs are different shapes and sizes.

When a herd of long-necked dinosaurs set off, the little ones walked in the middle, protected by the enormous grown-ups.

When Maiasaura babies
hatched out, their mother
brought them tender
young plants to eat.
After a few weeks,
the babies could look
for their own food.

A baby dinosaur curled
up inside its egg.

Nest built
inside
an earth
mound

Giants of the sea

While dinosaurs ruled the land, many fierce reptiles lived in the sea. Some of them were fast swimmers and looked like dolphins. Others were like lizards, or had strange long necks and giant flippers like paddles.

Kronosaurus had a huge head—bigger than a car.

Mosasaurus was a fierce sea lizard. It crushed small sea creatures in its powerful jaws.

Elasmosaurus had a long snakelike neck. It may have swum along holding its neck and tiny head above the water.

Ichthyosaurus looked like one of today's dolphins. It was a fast swimmer and may have hunted in shoals. It ate fish and creatures like squid.

Teleosaurus was a sea crocodile. It could quickly snap up fish in its long snout armed with sharp teeth.

Take to the skies

The first creatures to fly were insects, 300 million years ago. Later, reptiles called pterosaurs took to the air. They glided across the sky, soaring above the dinosaurs on the ground.

Archaeopteryx was the first creature with feathers. It was half dinosaur and half bird. No one knows if it could fly.

Quetzalcoatlus was a giant pterosaur, much, much bigger than even the largest birds today. Its huge wings were made of skin, like a bat's wings. It had a furry body and no feathers or teeth.

The first insects with wings were dragonflies. Meganeura was a huge dragonfly with a wingspan of about 30 inches.

FLY A PTEROSAUR

Take two dowels, one twice as long as the other, and tie together as shown. Get an adult to cut notches in the ends. Make a frame by tying string to each corner. Lay the frame on a clear plastic bag, and cut two inches around the it. Stretch the bag on the frame and tape the edges down. Cut out a pterosaur and tape it to the kite. Tie some string on it to fly the kite.

Fur and feathers

After the dinosaurs all died out, mammals and birds became more common. Unlike dinosaurs, both are warm-blooded. Mammals have fur or hair, and give birth to live babies. Birds have feathers to keep them warm.

Saghatherium was about the size of a lion, but very shy. It ate grass and had tiny hooves on its toes.

Not all mammals lived on land. Desmostylus looked a lot like a walrus and had long tusks. It spent most of its time hunting for fish in the sea, but came ashore to have its babies.

Hyracotherium was one of the first horses. It was very small, not much bigger than a cat. Instead of hooves, it had four toes on each front foot and three toes on its back feet.

Diatryma was a huge bird with a beak like a parrot's. It couldn't fly, but it could run fast.

Smilodon was a big, fierce, saber-toothed cat. It killed its victims by stabbing them with its daggerlike front teeth.

First people

For most of Earth's history, there have been no humans. The first people like us lived only about 100,000 years ago. They may have been related to apelike creatures that lived earlier.

People living 15,000 years ago survived by hunting, fishing, and gathering plants to eat. They moved from place to place in search of food, and took shelter in caves and tents.

Making a fire

Some people lived in caves in France. They painted pictures of the animals they hunted on their cave walls, using colors made from crushed rocks.

People hunted woolly mammoths. They were huge, and had long, thick hair to protect them from the icy cold weather.

Draw a big woolly mammoth on a large piece of construction paper, copying the picture on the right. Color in its tusks, toes, and eyes. To make its hairy coat, cut short pieces of reddish-brown yarn and glue them to the picture. If you want to, you can cut it out.

Making tools

Early people were good at making things with their hands. Remains found in their caves show that they made knives and weapons from sharp stones, and tools from antlers, bones, and mammoth tusks.

101

Plant Life

Food for growth

Plants need food and water to grow. Their roots take water from the soil and their leaves take in air and sunlight. Plants use water, air, and sunlight to make their own food.

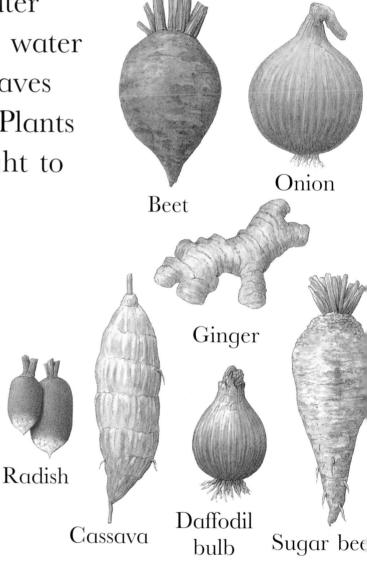

Beet

Onion

Ginger

Radish

Cassava

Daffodil bulb

Sugar bee

TAKE A CUTTING

Spider plants grow baby plants at the ends of long stems. Snip off a baby plant and put it in a glass of water. When it has grown roots, plant it in a small pot of moist soil.

All plants have roots. Some plants have fat roots, others have swollen buds or stems under the ground. These are used to store food. Plants use the food stored in them to grow when conditions are right.

Leaves breathe in carbon dioxide and breathe out oxygen.

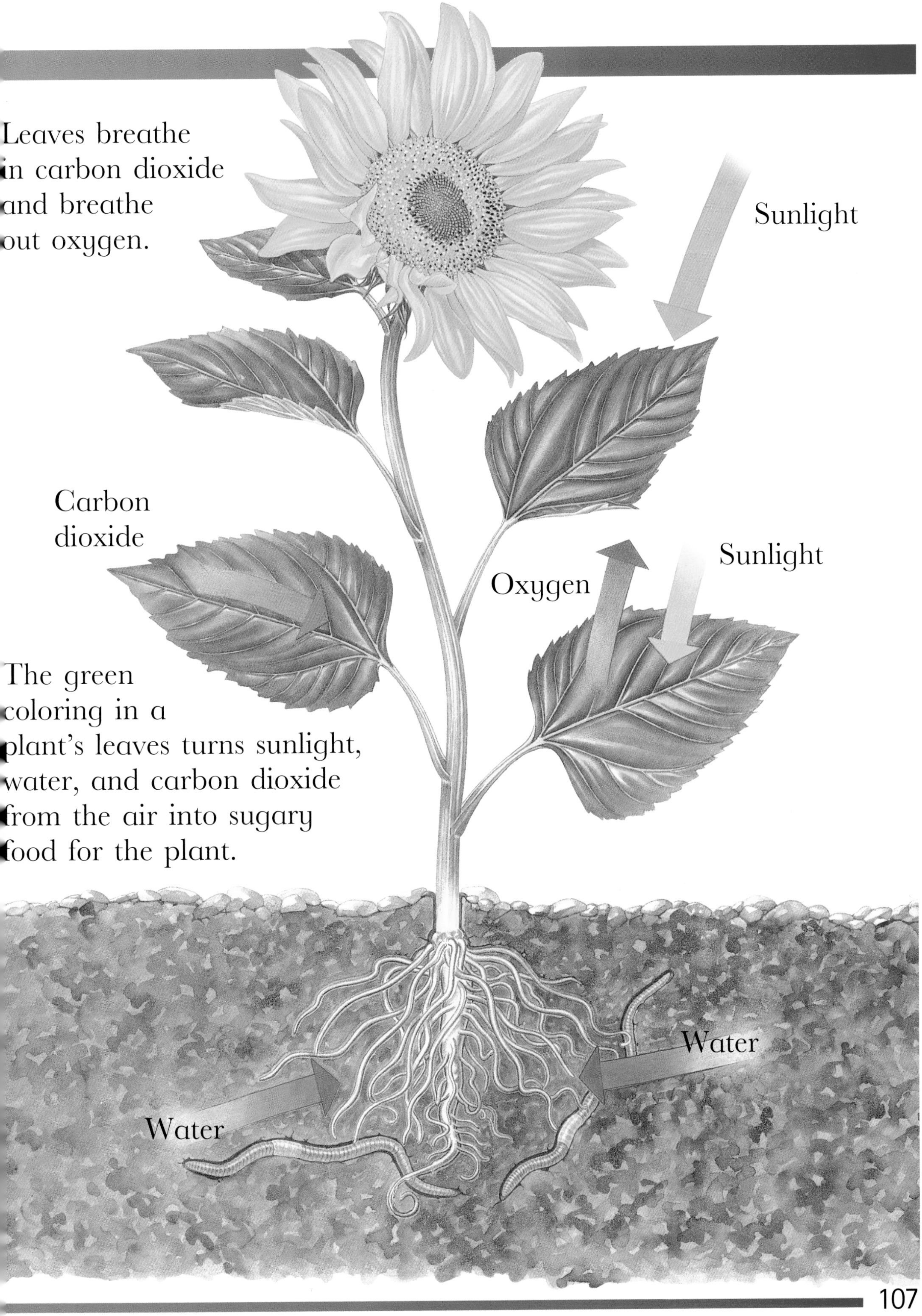

Sunlight

Carbon dioxide

Oxygen

Sunlight

The green coloring in a plant's leaves turns sunlight, water, and carbon dioxide from the air into sugary food for the plant.

Water

Water

Flowers

Flowers come in nearly every color, and many different shapes—bells, circles, stars, and trumpets. Garden flowers are often the showy relatives of simple wildflowers.

A meadow is full of flowers in the spring and summer. Butterflies and other insects visit the flowers because they like their color and scent.

Buttercups

Poppies

Some flowers, like this orchid, are rare and only grow in a few places. It is important not to pick rare plants so that they can make seeds for new plants.

Daisies

PRESS FLOWERS

Lay fresh flowers between pieces of newspaper in a book. Shut the book and put something heavy on top. Leave for four weeks, then use the flowers to decorate cards and bookmarks.

Clover

Making seeds

To make seeds, a flower needs pollen from another flower. Most flowers contain a sweet juice called nectar that birds and insects drink. As they drink, they brush against pollen, which they carry from flower to flower. This is called pollination.

Tiny hummingbirds pollinate some flowers in hot countries. They push their beaks right into the flowers to reach the nectar inside

Pollen

Hibiscus flowers attract hummingbirds.

Many flowers are pollinated by insects. The bee orchid tricks bees into thinking it is a female bee. Bees land on it and pick up the flower's sticky pollen.

Bee orchid

Flowers

Pollen

Catkins are male tree flowers. The wind blows clouds of catkin pollen to female tree flowers so that they can make seeds.

Catkins

Stigma

Petal

Anther covered in pollen

All flowers have the same parts. To make seeds, pollen is carried from the anthers of one flower to the stigma of another.

Seeds grow in the carpel.

Fruits and berries

After a flower has been pollinated, seeds start to grow. They are protected by a soft fruit which grows around the seeds. Some fruits only contain one big seed or stone. Berries have a lot of tiny seeds inside them.

In the fall, hedges are full of ripe, juicy berries. These are eaten by birds and animals. Later, the seeds inside the berries are scattered on the ground in bird and animal droppings.

Look for these berries in the picture:

1. Hawthorn berries
2. Rosehips
3. Blackberries
4. Elderberries
5. Rowan berries

Ask an adult to slice the top off a pumpkin. Scoop out the seeds and flesh. Cut holes in the pumpkin to make it look like a face. Wedge a short candle in the base of the pumpkin and ask an adult to light it for you.

4

5

All trees make fruits. These contain seeds that can grow into new trees. Some fruits, such as oranges, are soft. Nuts are tree fruits with hard shells around them.

Orange tree

Seeds

Most plants grow from seeds which fall on the ground. In the spring, the soil is damp and warm. This makes each seed swell and start to grow. The root grows first, then a shoot. This is called germination.

Seeds inside berries often reach the ground in bird droppings.

Dandelion seeds are blown to the ground by the wind.

Bean seed

Root / Shoot

When a seed germinates, it splits open and a root begins to grow. A leafy shoot pushes up through the soil toward the light. Leaves help the plant to make its own food.

First real leaves

Stem

MINIGARDEN

Wad some tissues into two clean eggshells. Sprinkle alfalfa seeds on top and keep the tissues damp. In ten days you will be able to cut some sprouts.

Some seeds are hidden inside soft, juicy fruit. Others have hard shells to protect them— these are called nuts.

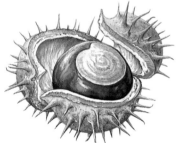

Horse chestnut

Peach

Pine cone

Sycamore

Trees

Trees are the biggest plants in the world. They have strong woody trunks and branches. There are two main kinds of tree. Deciduous trees lose their leaves in winter. Evergreens have leaves all year round.

Deciduous leaves often change color in the fall

Horse chestnut seed

Horse chestnut flowers

Deciduous trees, such as the horse chestnut, lose their leaves every fall and grow new ones in the spring. Horse chestnuts are green and leafy in summer and bare in winter.

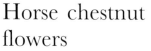

Horse chestnu

Tape a piece of paper to a tree. Rub a wax crayon up and down the paper, using the long side of the crayon.

Some evergreens are called conifers because they have cones.

Evergreens, such as the spruce, have long, thin leaves with a hard, waxy surface. These are called needles. They stay on the tree for several years before they drop off, though they never all fall off at the same time.

Spruce

117

Ferns and fungi

Ferns, fungi, mosses, and lichens are unusual plants. They do not have flowers and some of them do not have stems or roots. Instead of seeds, they make tiny spores that will grow into new plants.

The fly agaric toadstool is poisonous.

Puffball spores

Puffballs pop and blow out clouds of tiny spores.

Fungi, or toadstools, are not green and do not have leaves or roots. Unlike other plants, they do not make their own food. They send tiny hairs down into rotting plants or animal dung so that they can feed on them.

Ferns grow in damp, shady places. They range in size from tiny mosslike plants to huge tree ferns. Ferns produce small, round spores underneath their leaves.

A fern frond slowly unfurls as it grows bigger.

Carpets of moss grow in damp places. Up close, the moss looks like forests of tiny stems and leaves.

Crusty lichens grow on trees, rocks, and old stonework. They grow very, very slowly.

Water plants

Many different plants live in water. They grow in rivers, ponds, lakes, and even in the sea. Most of them are rooted in the mud under the water. Some water plants are huge, while others can only be seen using a microscope.

Tall reeds grow along the edges of rivers and lakes. Water lilies grow closer to the middle. Their stems grow up through the water and their big, flat leaves and flowers float on the surface.

Common reed

Water lily

Mangrove trees grow in saltwater swamps in hot countries. Their roots are like giant stilts. The roots hold the tree in place and keep its branches above the water.

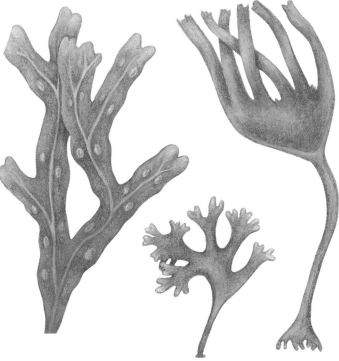

Green, red, and brown seaweed grows along rocky shores. They do not grow in the seabed, but cling to rocks instead. Seaweeds get their food from seawater. They soak this up with their rubbery branches, called fronds.

The Amazonian water lily grows along the Amazon River in South America. Its enormous floating leaves can be up to six feet wide.

Plants and animals

Without plants, there would not be any animals. Plants provide all kinds of animals with food and homes. In return, animals help to scatter the seeds that will grow into new plants.

Harvest mouse

Harvest mice eat grass seeds, like a lot of other small animals. The spiky seedheads of some plants stick to their fur and are carried to different places, where the seeds fall off and grow.

Some animals eat only one kind of food. Koalas live in eucalyptus trees in Australia. They eat nothing but the juicy eucalyptus leaves.

Goldfinches also feed on seeds. They crush them in their beaks. Some of the seeds are scattered on the ground in bird droppings.

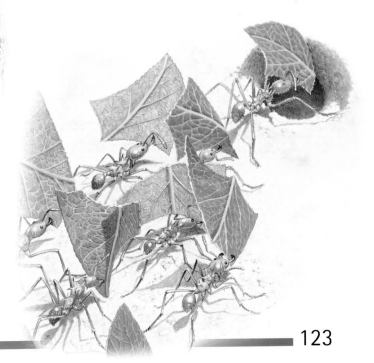

Leaf-cutter ants snip up leaves and carry them to their nest, where they chew them into a pulp. The ants feed on fungus that grows on the leaves.

Plant meat-eaters

There are some very strange plants that eat meat. Insects that land on them looking for nectar find themselves caught in the plants' clever traps. Juices from the plants slowly turn the insects' bodies into liquid, and the plants soak up the liquid food.

The leaves of the sundew plant are covered in sticky hairs. When an insect lands on a leaf, it gets stuck to the hairs and cannot escape.

Venus flytrap

Sundew

The sundew leaf slowly folds over the insect to trap it.

124

The Venus flytrap moves quickly to catch insects. When an insect lands on one of its open leaf pads, it brushes against tiny hairs. These make the leaf pads snap shut, like a trap, so that the insect cannot escape.

Lid to keep rain out

Closed leaf pad

Open leaf pad

Pitcher plant

The pitcher plant has pitcherlike traps at the ends of its leaves. Each pitcher has slippery edges and is half full of liquid. Insects fall into the liquid and drown.

Plant defenses

Plants are always under attack from hungry animals. They cannot run away, so they have different ways of protecting themselves. Some plants have thorns or spines. Others are poisonous or taste bad.

If the leaves of poison ivy are damaged, milky juice leaks out of them. This juice makes animals' skin itch and gives them painful blisters.

Cacti are juicy inside because they store water and food in their stems and leaves. They have sharp spines to protect them from thirsty desert animals.

Giraffes can stretch their necks high into trees to reach food. They like to eat the tender leaves and shoots growing on acacia trees. The acacia tree has tough, sharp thorns that stop other animals from eating it.

Some nettle leaves are covered with tiny spines. If an animal brushes against the plant, its spines pierce the animal's skin and inject it with painful chemicals.

Plants called "living stones" use camouflage to protect themselves from animals. Their leaves look like the stones around them, so that they are hard to spot.

127

Unusual plants

Some plants are very unusual. They might be a strange shape, have a peculiar smell, or grow to an enormous size. Others look normal, but they live in places where no other plants can survive.

The rafflesia is the biggest flower in the world, measuring nearly three feet across. It smells of rotting meat to attract the flies that pollinate it.

In some deserts, flowers burst into bloom only after it rains. They quickly make seeds, then die. The seeds sometimes lie in the ground for many years until it rains again.

Bonsai trees are very small. They look just like normal trees, but some are only a little bit bigger than a butterfly. Bonsai trees do not grow like this naturally. People trim their roots to keep them from growing any bigger.

The largest and the oldest living things on Earth are the giant redwood trees of California. The tallest tree is over 370 feet high. Its trunk is more than 80 feet thick.

Giant redwood

131

Animal World

What is a reptile?

Snakes, lizards, crocodiles, and turtles are all reptiles. They have dry, scaly skin. Reptiles are cold-blooded. This means that their bodies are the same temperature as their surroundings. They lie in the sun to warm up, then hide in the shade to cool down.

Most reptiles hatch from eggs, like this baby snake. Reptile eggs do not have hard shells. Instead, they are soft and leathery.

Gecko

Snakes and lizards, such as this gecko, shed their skins as they grow. A new layer of skin is ready underneath.

A snake does not smell things with its nose, but with its forked tongue. It flickers its tongue in and out to track down food.

Forked tongue

The frilled lizard spreads out its neck frill to make itself look very fierce and frighten away enemies.

Frilled lizard

Lizards

Geckos, iguanas, skinks, and chameleons are all lizards. They usually live on the ground, but some spend their lives scuttling in the treetops or burrowing underground. Most lizards eat insects.

Many lizards are brightly colored and patterned. This eyed lizard gets its name from the blue spots along its sides.

The Gila monster is a poisonous lizard. It makes poison in its mouth and bites small animals to kill them.

138

The horned lizard looks scary, but it is actually harmless.

A chameleon is a type of tree lizard whose tongue is as long as its body. It shoots its tongue out very fast to catch insects.

The Komodo dragon (below) is the largest lizard in the world, and very fierce. It has sharp, jagged teeth, a bit like a shark's.

Chameleon

Komodo dragon

The chameleon changes color to match the things around it. This makes it hard to spot in the treetops.

Turtles

Turtles and tortoises are the only reptiles with a heavy shell to protect them from enemies. Some turtles live on land, and some in the sea or in fresh water. Tortoises live only on land. Turtles and tortoises both lay their eggs on land.

2. The turtle digs a hole. She lays her eggs in it and covers them with sand.

3. When the baby turtles hatch, they climb out of the sand and run to the sea.

1. A turtle swims to a sandy beach at night to lay her eggs.

A tortoise moves very slowly. When something scares it, it tucks its head and legs right inside its shell.

MAKE A TURTLE

Make a hole in each side of a styrofoam bowl. Thread some elastic through the holes and tie the ends. Glue brown paper patches around the bottom of the bowl. Glue paper eyes to the middle finger of a glove. Put on the glove and wear the bowl on top.

Giant tortoises live on the Galapagos Islands. They may live for up to 50 years and grow to be three feet long.

Crocodiles

Crocodiles usually live in rivers in hot countries. They spend most of their time lying in the water, waiting for animals to come to drink. Then they lunge forward to attack. Few animals can escape their sharp teeth.

Crocodiles float with their eyes and nose above the surface.

Alligator

Garial

Caiman

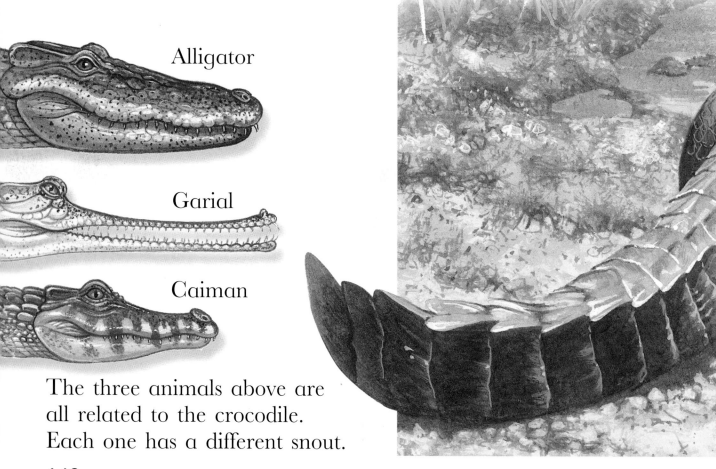

The three animals above are all related to the crocodile. Each one has a different snout.

142

An alligator (above) lies on a sunny riverbank to warm up. It cools down by rolling around in deep pools of water.

A mother crocodile (below) looks after her eggs. When they hatch, she carries the babies gently down to the river in her huge mouth.

Amphibians

Most amphibians are born in water, but live on land when they are adults. Frogs, toads, salamanders, newts, and caecilians are all amphibians. They eat insects, snails, and other small animals.

Frogs have smooth, slimy skin and long back legs. They are good at jumping and swimming.

Great crested newt

Newts spend part of the year on land. They usually sleep all through the cold winter. In the spring they find a pond to lay their eggs.

Toads are chubbier than frogs and have dry, lumpy skin. They have shorter legs than frogs and waddle around quite slowly.

The caecilian looks like a worm, but has sharp teeth. It lives in tropical rain forests and burrows in the leaf litter on the ground.

Like newts, salamanders have long tails. They are shy animals that hide in damp places under logs or rocks.

Frogs

Frogs live in many different places. Some can even be found high up in the treetops. All frogs lay their eggs in water. The tiny creatures that hatch do not look like frogs at first, but they change as they grow. This is called metamorphosis.

A frog can leap a long way because its back legs are like springs. It starts with them folded. To jump, it unfolds its long back legs and springs forward.

1. A frog lays hundreds of eggs. The eggs are laid in a clear jelly. These are known as frogspawn.

Mother frog

2. Tadpoles grow inside the eggs.

Tree frogs have sticky pads on their fingers and toes to help them grip tree branches.

FROG LEAPS

See if you can jump like a frog. Squat down and put your hands on the floor between your feet. Take a giant leap forward and land in the same position. Why not have a frog race with your friends?

3. The eggs hatch into tadpoles.

5. The tadpoles turn into frogs and leave the water.

4. The tadpoles grow bigger and develop legs.

What is a fish?

Fish live in water and are amazing swimmers. Some fish are as small as tadpoles and others longer than crocodiles. Some are flat and others tube-shaped. But most fish have the same basic features.

Slippery scales on a fish's body help it to glide smoothly through the water.

Most fish lay eggs. They lay hundreds of tiny eggs at a time.

Fish use their fins to steer and turn as they swim.

A fish does not have eyelids, so it always swims with its eyes wide open.

Some fish live in the sea, where the water is salty. Others live in rivers and lakes. These are called freshwater fish.

Fish have slits called gills on the sides of their heads so that they can breathe under water.

A fish swims along by beating its tail from side to side.

AN AQUARIUM

Paint the inside of a shoebox blue-green. Turn the box onto its side and put pebbles and shells inside it. Draw, color, and cut out some pretty fish. Tape a string to each fish and tape them to the top of the box.

Coral fish

Thousands of brightly colored fish dart through the clear blue waters around a coral reef. Corals grow in many shapes and colors, like a rocky garden under the sea. The water is shallow and sunny, and there is plenty to eat.

Most of the fish that live on coral reefs have colorful spots or stripes. This makes it hard for a hunter to spot them swimming through the corals.

1. Trumpet fish
2. Cowfish
3. Parrot fish
4. Butterfly fish
5. Lion fish
6. Angel fish

Sea hunters

Many of the creatures that live in the sea feed on plants, but others are fierce and deadly hunters. Some sea hunters rely on speed to catch their prey, but others have more unusual ways of finding their food.

The great white shark hunts by scent. When the shark smells food, it charges toward it with amazing speed. The shark snaps its prey up in its huge jaws and swallows it whole.

152

The whale shark
is the biggest fish in the
world, but it only feeds on
the tiniest sea creatures,
called plankton.

An octopus slithers
along the seabed and
grabs shellfish with one
of its eight long arms.

The Portuguese
man-of-war trails
its long, stinging
tentacles through
the water to
catch fish.

Octopus

153

Deep-sea fish

In the deepest parts of the sea, the water is pitch-dark and freezing cold. No plants grow and there is hardly any food, but some very strange creatures still manage to live there.

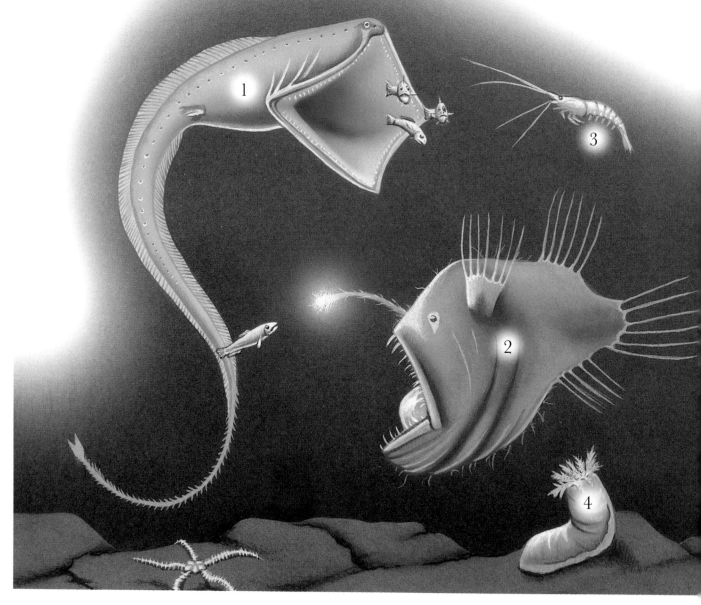

Many of the fish that live in the deepest part of the sea are black, so they are very hard to see. Some of them have tiny lights on their bodies. These attract smaller fish, which make tasty food. The lights also act as a signal to help them to find a mate.

1. Gulper eel
2. Anglerfish
3. Deep-sea shrimp
4. Sea cucumber
5. Flashlight fish
6. Tripod fish
7. Brittle star

What is an insect?

Most insects are small. Their bodies are made up of three parts—a head, a thorax (middle), and an abdomen (back part). An insect has six legs and two antennae. Its body is protected by a hard outer case.

Thorax

Head

Proboscis

Antennae

The wings of the brightly colored shield bug are hidden beneath the large striped shield on its back.

Honeybees feed on nectar, a sweet juice inside flowers. They suck up the nectar through a feeding tube called a proboscis. Honeybees also collect flower pollen.

Ants live in colonies.

A butterfly has four wings. It folds them above its back when resting.

Wing

Abdomen

This leaf insect looks just like the leaf it is sitting on. It is very hard for hungry animals to see it.

Tiny clawed leg

A stick insect looks like a twig.

Termites live in huge groups called colonies. Their giant nests, made of mud and sand, protect the queen termite in the middle.

Termite

Butterflies

On a warm summer day, butterflies flutter from flower to flower, feeding on nectar. The beautiful patterns on a butterfly's wings are made of thousands of brightly colored, overlapping scales. Moths are like butterflies, but fly at night.

Monarch butterfly

A butterfly begins life as a wriggly caterpillar. It has to change completely before it becomes a butterfly.

1. A butterfly lays its eggs on a plant.

2. The eggs hatch into caterpillars.

3. The caterpillars eat and grow bigger.

Tiger moth

Moths have fatter bodies than butterflies and their antennae are not as thick as butterfly antennae. Moth antennae are feathery or look like hairs.

The death's-head moth has a shape like a skull on the back of its head.

Cinnabar moth

4. Each caterpillar turns into a pupa.

5. A butterfly breaks out of the pupa.

Minimonsters

There are many tiny creatures that are not insects and cannot fly. Most of them hide away among plants or stones during the day. They usually come out to look for food at night, or just after it has rained.

An earthworm eats the soil as it wriggles its way through. It has no eyes, ears, or legs.

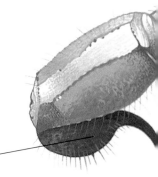

Stinger

Scorpions usually live in hot countries. They are very fierce. A scorpion catches its prey in its giant pincers and kills it with the poisonous stinger at the end of its tail.

Pincer

The hairy tarantula is one of the biggest spiders in the world.

A centipede has a lot of tiny legs. There is one pair of legs on each segment of its body.

HAIRY SPIDER

Make a pompom by winding yarn around two cardboard disks with holes in the middle. Push four pipe cleaners through the holes. Cut around the edge of the cardboard and tie some yarn around the middle. Take out the cardboard. Bend the pipe cleaners to make legs, and stick on eyes.

Snails slither along the ground, leaving trails of slime behind them. If they are scared, they quickly draw back into their shells.

163

Birds and Mammals

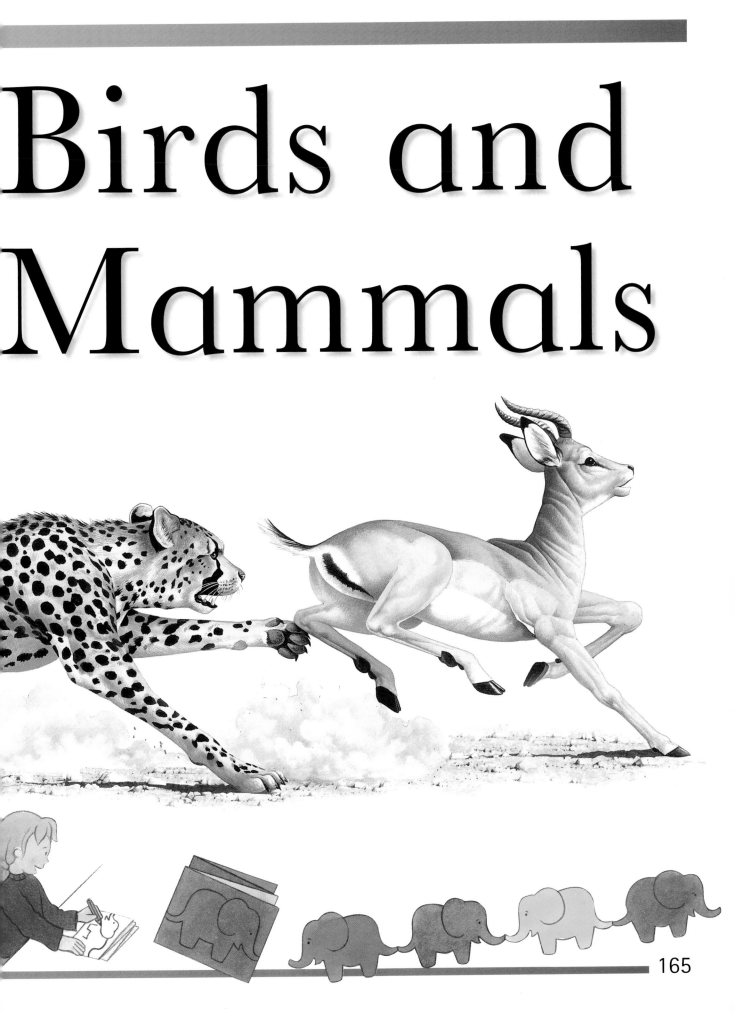

What is a bird?

There are thousands of different birds of every color, shape, and size. Birds are the only animals that have feathers, and most birds can fly. The smallest bird is no bigger than a butterfly. The largest is taller than a man.

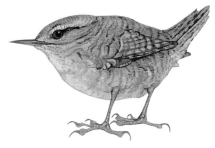

The tiny wren is only about as long as your finger.

A bird's body is a clever flying machine. Birds have very light bones and strong wing muscles to make it easier to fly. Their feathers keep them warm and dry. A bird's tail helps it to steer and brake when it is flying.

The shape
of a bird's beak
shows what kind of food it
eats. The toucan's giant bill
is good for plucking fruit.

The ostrich cannot fly.
It is the biggest and
heaviest bird of all.

The peregrine's smooth shape
helps it to fly and dive very fast.

Flying

Birds are amazing acrobats. They can swoop, glide, and hover in the air. Bats and insects fly too, but birds can fly faster, higher, and farther. Some of them are so good at flying that they can stay in the air for years.

A bird flaps its wings up and down to fly. Big birds flap their wings slowly. Small birds flap theirs fast.

Flight feathers are very smooth

Kingfisher

Soft, downy feathers keep the body warm

Different birds have different shaped wings, to suit the way they live. A kingfisher has short, stubby wings. Strong wings like this help the kingfisher to get back into the air from water after diving.

Contour feathers give the body a streamlined shape

A goose lifts its wings right up above its back.

Then it pulls its wings down again.

The albatross glides through the skies on huge wings over ten feet across. The wings are narrow and the same shape as a glider's.

Tiny hummingbirds hover while they suck nectar from flowers. They beat their wings very fast—50 to 80 times a second. This makes a loud humming sound.

MAKE A FLYING DUCK

Draw the outline of a duck on construction paper. Color in both sides and cut it out. Draw and cut out two wings with tabs, as shown. Fold the wings along the dotted lines. Glue the wings to the duck. Hang it from a piece of thin elastic.

Birds of prey

Birds of prey are fierce hunters with sharp beaks and claws, and very good eyesight. They soar high in the sky, hunting for small animals or fish. When they spot an animal moving beneath them, they swoop down from the sky and kill it.

Eagles are the biggest birds of prey. They have long, sharp claws called talons, and they attack feetfirst. The bald eagle catches fish. It swoops down to the water, grabs a fish and carries it away.

Owls hunt at night and can see well even in the dark. Fringed feathers at the edges of their wings help them fly without a sound.

Groups of vultures gather at a kill. Vultures are scavengers. They usually eat animals that are already dead.

BEAKY BIRD CARD

Fold some construction paper in half and cut a slit in the middle. Fold back the corners and push them inside out. Glue the card to more

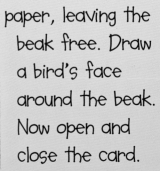

paper, leaving the beak free. Draw a bird's face around the beak. Now open and close the card.

Water birds

Many birds live near water. Some of them are good at swimming and some just wade at the water's edge. Seabirds feed on fish from the sea. Other birds nest close to rivers or lakes, where there is also plenty of food.

Ducks, geese, swans, and most seabirds have webbed feet. These help them swim quickly.

Puffins dive into the sea to catch fish. Their colorful beaks are so big that they can hold several small fish at a time. Huge groups of puffins make their nests on steep cliffs.

The heron has long legs like stilts and a sharp beak like a dagger. It stands very still at the edge of a river or lake, waiting for fish. When the heron spots one, it stabs it with its beak and gulps it down.

The arctic tern travels farther than any other bird. It nests near the North Pole, then flies to the South Pole at the other end of the world for the winter. In the spring, it flies all the way back to the North Pole again.

Penguins fish in the icy cold seas near the South Pole. They have short wings like flippers and swim so fast that they look as if they are flying through the water.

Nests and eggs

All birds lay eggs that hatch into chicks. Most birds make soft nests in which to lay their eggs. They build them in safe places, away from enemies. Then the birds sit on their eggs to keep them warm until they hatch.

When a chick is ready to hatch, it uses a special tooth to chip a hole in its shell. When the hole is big enough, the chick pushes its way out, headfirst.

Crows build big, messy nests high in treetops. The nests are made of sticks bound together with mud and moss. Inside, they are lined with a thick layer of soft wool or hair.

The chicks squawk for food.

The Indian tailor bird makes its nest by sewing leaves together with silk from a spider's web.

Swallows build cup-shaped mud nests high up on walls, out of reach of enemies.

The chicks are covered in fluffy down.

The plover does not make a nest. Instead, it lays its eggs on gravel, where the speckled eggs are well camouflaged.

Apes and monkeys

Apes, monkeys, and humans all belong to a group of animals called primates. The easiest way to tell an ape from a monkey is to look for a tail— a monkey has one, but an ape does not. Gorillas are the largest apes of all.

Gorillas are shy, gentle creatures. They live in family groups and like playing together.

Howler monkeys make one of the loudest animal sounds.

178

Orangutans live alone, but they care for their babies just like humans.

MONKEY CHAIN

Trace the monkey shape above several times on construction paper and cut out the shapes. Hook the arms and tails of the monkeys together into a chain.

Hunting

Many mammals are meat-eaters. This means that they have to catch other animals to eat. Animal hunters are armed with sharp teeth and claws, and can usually run very fast. Some animals hunt alone. Others work together to track down their prey.

Wolves and other wild dogs hunt in groups called packs. Each pack has a strong dog as a leader. Wolves work as a team to catch large animals.

The cheetah can run faster than any other animal. It silently slinks as close as it can to its prey, then sprints forwards and takes it by surprise.

Bears kill other animals with a swipe of their massive paws. The brown bear likes fish. It hooks salmon out of the water as they swim upstream to lay their eggs.

Living in a herd

Animals that eat plants spend most of their time grazing on grass or munching leaves. Many of them live on grasslands where there is nowhere to hide from hunters. It is safer for them to live together in large herds.

Wild horses move from place to place in herds. Each herd is made up of female horses and their foals. They are led by a stallion, a male horse.

Mother elephants and their babies live together in family groups, led by an older female. All the adults help take care of the babies.

Wildebeest live in enormous herds. Each herd travels great distances, looking for fresh grass to eat.

MAKE AN ELEPHANT CHAIN

Fold a long piece of paper into wide pleats. Draw an elephant on the top fold, with its trunk and tail touching each side, as shown. Cut out the elephant and unfold the paper to make an elephant chain.

Rodents

Rodents are mammals with big, sharp front teeth. They use them for gnawing and chewing things. Some rodents eat grasses, roots, and tough seeds. Others will eat anything that they can find.

A squirrel often perches on the same spot to eat. It holds nuts or tree seeds in its front paws and cracks them open with its strong teeth.

Rats live in large groups called colonies. They live near water, on garbage dumps, in old buildings, and even in people's homes. Rats eat anything. They will chew their way through wires, walls, wood, and plastic.

184

FINGER MOUSE

Make two cardboard ears. Find two black beads and three twist ties. Twist the ties as shown. Draw a nose and mouth on the finger of a glove with a pen. Glue ears to the back. Sew on beads for eyes and ties for whiskers.

Beavers are great builders. They gnaw around trees to make them fall down and use the wood to dam a stream. Then they build a home out of branches and twigs in the middle of the pond they have made.

Marmots are furry rodents that live high in the mountains. Large family groups live in burrows under the ground. In winter, they block the entrances to their burrows and sleep until spring.

185

Marsupials

Marsupials are mammals with a pouch that their babies grow in. The babies are very small when they are born. They crawl up into their mother's pouch and live there until they are bigger.

Kangaroos live in Australia. They have strong back legs and hop very fast along the ground, using their tails to keep their balance. A baby kangaroo is called a joey. It is no bigger than a fingernail when it is born. It stays in its mother's pouch for nine months or more.

Koalas are not bears. They are related to opossums. Koalas live in eucalyptus trees in Australia. Eucalyptus leaves are the only thing they eat. The leaves are so juicy that koalas never need to drink.

The Australian possum lives in trees. Baby possums live for 10 weeks in their mother's pouch, then they climb out and cling tightly to her fur.

ROO PENCIL POUCH

Draw a big kangaroo outline on felt and cut it out. Cut out two ears and a pouch. Glue the ears to the kangaroo and sew on the pouch. Draw a face and arms. Glue on beads for eyes.

Water mammals

Some mammals spend most of their time in water. All water mammals are very good swimmers. Many of them dive deep underwater to catch fish. They can stay there for a long time, but they have to return to the surface to breathe.

Otters live by rivers and seas. They have thick waterproof fur to keep them warm when they swim in cold water.

Hippotamuses live in Africa. During the day they stay in rivers and lakes to keep cool. At night they go ashore to find grass and plants to eat.

The blue whale is the biggest animal in the world. It eats tiny shrimp called krill. It sieves them out of the water through a bony fringe in its mouth called a baleen.

Seals live in cold seas. They have a thick layer of fat called blubber to keep them warm. Seals have flippers instead of back legs. They are fast swimmers and chase after fish, squid, and octopus.

Strange mammals

From the tiniest mouse to the biggest whale, mammals come in every shape and size, and some of them are pretty strange.

The armadillo curls up when it is in danger. Its body is protected by bony plates of armor.

The aardvark lives on African grasslands. It eats insects called termites. When it finds a termite mound, it rips it open with its sharp claws and licks up the insects with its long, sticky tongue.

INVENT AN ANIMAL

The giraffe has long legs and a very long neck. It can stretch right up into the trees, to pull off juicy leaves and shoots that other animals cannot reach.

Fold a long piece of paper into sections, as shown below. With a friend, take turns to draw part of a different animal on each section. When you open the paper out, you will see the animal you have invented!

The platypus is furry. But it also has a flat beak and webbed feet, like a duck. It is the only mammal that lays eggs.

Animals in danger

Sadly, some animals are in danger of dying out forever. Thousands of animals die every year because their homes are destroyed when forests are chopped down. Other animals are killed by hunters.

Great auks are extinct now. "Extinct" means that an animal has died out. Great auks were hunted for food until there were none left.

Tigers were in danger of dying out in India a few years ago, so a campaign was launched to save them. Special wildlife parks were set up where tigers can live safely.

192

The giant panda is one of the rarest animals in the world. There are fewer than 1,000 of them left. Pandas live in lonely parts of China. They only eat bamboo. Every few years the bamboo dies off. Some pandas die because they cannot find enough food.

The black rhinoceros lives in Africa and feeds on leaves and twigs. For a long time hunters have killed rhinos for their horns, which are used to make Asian medicines. Now it is against the law to hunt rhinos.

Different people

There are millions of people in the world, and they are all different shapes, sizes, and colors. But underneath their skin, everyone's body is made up of the same parts and works in the same way.

Think about all the people that you know. No two are exactly the same. Out of all the people in the world, there is no one exactly like you.

The only people who look the same as each other are identical twins. They are always either both girls or both boys. Non-identical twins just look like brother and sister, sister and sister, or brother and brother.

Your body is much smaller than an adult's, but it is basically the same. As you grow, the different parts of your body grow, too. Some of them also change a little as you become an adult.

Inside you

Inside your body there are parts called organs that are hard at work all the time. Each organ does a special job that keeps your body working correctly. They all work together like the different parts of a machine.

Your brain, lungs, heart, liver, stomach, and intestines are organs. They receive all the things they need from your blood, as it flows around your body.

Brain

Lungs

Heart

Liver

Stomach

Intestines

198

Your heart pumps your blood around every part of your body. It beats about 70 times a minute all the time you are alive.

Lay two fingers gently on the inside of your other wrist, below the creases. Count how many beats you feel in 15 seconds. Multiply this by four to find out how often your heart beats in a minute.

Your heart is about the same size as your clenched fist. As you grow, your heart grows bigger and stronger, too.

Bones and joints

There are more than 200 bones that together make up your skeleton. This strong framework supports and protects the soft parts of your body. Without it, you would not be able to stand up or move around.

Skull

Ribcage

Spine

Pelvis

Bones are different shapes and sizes, depending on the job they do. Your skull forms a strong, bony case around your delicate brain. Your ribcage surrounds your chest to protect the organs inside.

The place where two bones meet is called a joint. The ends of the bones fit together or slide over each other smoothly.

Basketball

Your joints allow you to perform many different activities.

Soccer

Draw a body, arms, and legs like these on black construction paper and cut them out. Make small holes with a pencil point where shown. Attach the arms and legs to the body with paper fasteners. Paint a skeleton on the body, using white paint. Hang the skeleton from a piece of string to scare your friends!

Bicycling

Ballet

Tennis

Baseball

These children are bending and stretching their bodies in all kinds of sports.

201

Skin and hair

Your body is snugly wrapped up in your skin. Skin is a stretchy, waterproof covering that fits you like a glove. It protects your insides from dirt and germs, and helps to keep your body at the right temperature.

The skin on your fingertips has tiny ridges on it. These help you to grip things. Everyone has a different pattern of ridges.

Skin is not always the same color. A brown coloring called melanin helps protect skin from sunlight. Brown skin contains more melanin than white skin. People from hot, sunny places often have dark skin.

You are always growing new skin, because skin wears away. Hairs grow from the lower layer of your skin. Nerve endings help you feel things. Sweat glands release sweat through tiny holes called pores. This cools you down.

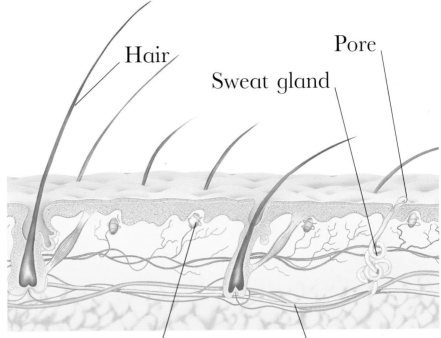

Hair

Sweat gland

Pore

Nerve ending

Blood vessels

DETECTIVE WORK

To take your fingerprints, roll each finger lightly on an ink pad, then press it firmly on a piece of paper. (Ask an adult to help.) Look at the patterns in each print with a magnifying glass.

When you are cold, you look pale because the blood vessels in your skin narrow to keep you from losing more heat. Your hairs stand on end to trap body heat, and you shiver to warm up.

The brain

Your brain is the control center of your whole body. It keeps all the different parts working, and it never shuts down. Every time you move, your brain sends a message to part of your body, telling it what to do. You also use your brain to think and feel.

Your nerves are like a system of wires that run from your brain all around your body. They carry millions of messages between your brain and the rest of your body.

Nerves carry messages at very high speed, so that you can react quickly to whatever is happening around you

Your brain is connectd to your nerves by your spinal cord. It runs down the middle of your spine.

TEST YOUR REACTIONS

Draw around a ruler on a piece of cardboard. Cut it out and mark six bands 2 inches wide. Color them as shown. Ask a friend to hold the ruler so that the red end is between your thumb and finger. Use the colored bands to work out how quickly you can catch the ruler when your friend drops it suddenly.

Your brain is inside your skull, to protect it.

Muscles

You have more than 600 muscles that help you move every part of your body. Every time you jump, chew, or just blink, you use different muscles. The brain controls all the muscles in your body, even when you are asleep.

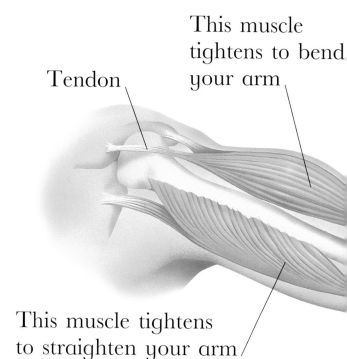

Tendon

This muscle tightens to bend your arm

This muscle tightens to straighten your arm

Muscles are joined to bones by cords of tissue called tendons. Muscles tighten to move bones. They only pull, so they usually work in pairs.

This gymnast is using hundreds of different muscles. She exercises to make her muscles stronger so she can bend, stretch, and jump more easily.

FUNNY FACE TRICKS

Some of the tiny muscles in your face are very hard to use. Have a competition with your friends to see who can waggle their ears, flare their nostrils, or arch their eyebrows—without moving any other part of their face at the same time.

Muscles in your face are hard at work all the time. Tiny muscles in your eyelids tighten to make you blink and wash your eyes with tears. You do this about 20,000 times a day!

Breathing

You breathe all the time, even when you are asleep. The air that you breathe into your lungs contains a gas called oxygen, which you need to stay alive. Your lungs take oxygen from the air, then your blood carries it all around your body.

Windpipe

Lungs

Your lungs are like big sponges. When you breathe in, they fill with air. When you breathe out or blow, they push out a waste gas called carbon dioxide that your body doesn't need.

People cannot breathe underwater or in space because there is no air. Divers wear oxygen tanks on their backs. They breathe in and out through tubes connected to the tank.

If there is something blocking or tickling your nose, you sneeze to blow out all the dust and germs. When you cough, your body is getting rid of any dust or germs that have entered your lungs.

209

The senses

You use your eyes, ears, nose, skin, and tongue to find out about the world around you. You look around and you listen, smell, touch, and taste things. You are using your five senses.

You feel things with your skin. The skin on fingertips is very sensitive. People who cannot see, "read" special raised text, called braille, with their fingertips.

Think how hard it is to walk when you are blindfolded. Your eyes give you a lot of useful information. Your ears are able to pick up a huge range of sounds.

You taste things with your tongue, but your nose helps, too. It is hard to taste something properly unless you can smell it, too.

Smells float in the air and are picked up by your nose when you breathe in. You can tell the difference between thousands of different smells. Some things smell nice and others smell very bad.

Your mouth

You use your mouth to eat and to speak. Your teeth chop up your food and your tongue helps you swallow it. When you speak or sing, your lips, tongue, and teeth shape the sounds you make.

The teeth you grew as a baby are called milk teeth. When you are about six, your milk teeth start to fall out. Bigger teeth grow in their place.

The surface of your tongue is covered with little bumps called taste buds. The taste buds on the back, sides, and tip of your tongue all pick up different kinds of tastes.

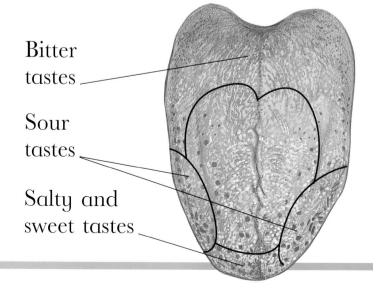

Bitter tastes

Sour tastes

Salty and sweet tastes

ACID ATTACK!

Ask an adult to hard-boil an egg. Put it in a glass and cover it with vinegar. Leave it for two days, then see how much of the eggshell has been eaten away by the vinegar. This is what candy and soft drinks do to your teeth.

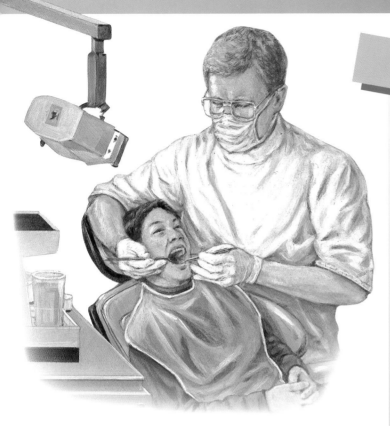

Dentists help you take care of your teeth. When you visit a dentist, they check that your teeth are healthy and growing correctly. They also repair teeth that are damaged.

You need to brush your teeth regularly to keep them healthy. If you do not, pieces of food and germs build up on your teeth to form an acid mixture called plaque. Plaque eats away at your teeth and gives you a toothache.

Eating

The food you eat should give you all you need to live and grow. You need to eat many different kinds of food to stay strong and healthy, because they contain the different things that are important for your body.

Fresh fruits and vegetables are packed with vitamins and minerals, and other things your body needs.

Your body takes all the energy you need to work and play from your food. This is why you need to eat regular meals throughout the day.

KEEP A FOOD DIARY

Draw a chart like this on a big piece of paper. Then write down what you eat at each meal every day for a week. How many different types of food do you eat?

Monday
Tuesday
Wednesday
Thursday
Friday
Saturday
Sunday

Throat

Stomach

Small intestine

Large intestine

After you swallow food, it travels down your throat to your stomach. It is turned into a mushy mass, then moves along your intestine. All the useful bits of food pass through the wall of your intestines into your blood.

When you are sick

Sometimes you get sick. You might have a cough, a high temperature, spots, or aches and pains. These are all signs that your body is trying to fight off an infection. Infections are caused by harmful germs too small to see.

Some diseases, such as chicken pox, are infectious. This means that they are easy to catch. But after you have had them once, you usually do not catch them again.

Sometimes when you are sick, you might be examined by a doctor. Doctors ask questions, listen to your heart and lungs, and look in your ears, eyes, and throat. They may give you medicine to help make you better.

There are many tablets and medicines for different sicknesses. Some medicines are given as injections. People with asthma use inhalers to help them breathe more easily.

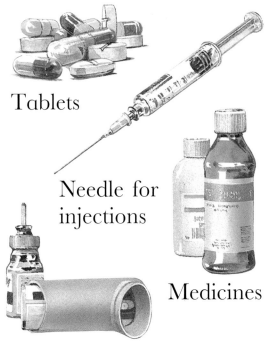

Tablets

Needle for injections

Inhaler

Medicines

If someone has an accident or is very sick, they go to the hospital. They may have an operation so that doctors can fix the part of the body that is damaged. They stay in the hospital until they are well.

Around the world

There are billions of people living on Earth. They live in different countries and speak many languages. People often do the same things, but they may have different customs and traditions.

These children come from all over the world. They are holding their countries' flags. Every country has its own flag, sometimes with a symbol of the country on it. A symbol is a picture or pattern that means something special to people.

Every country has its own stamps. They often show interesting things from that country.

China

Greece

Brazil

Sweden

Germany

Israel

226

Every country uses its own type of money, called currency. The money is usually paper bills and coins. These often show pictures of people who are important in that country.

227

Where you live

Whether you live in a city or in the country, there will be a map of the area. Maps show what places look like from above. The maps are much smaller than the places they show, but they tell you a lot about them.

Imagine how a bird sees a city from up in the air. Everything looks a different shape from above.

This is a map of the city from a bird's-eye view. The map shows the streets, pond, and buildings as shapes. Everything is drawn to scale—it is the right size compared to everything else.

MAP YOUR BEDROOM

Bedroom

Map

Draw a map of your bedroom. Pretend you are a fly on your bedroom ceiling, and draw simple shapes to show the furniture. To make everything the right size, measure your room and furniture in footsteps. Then draw your map on graph paper, pretending that each square has sides one footstep long.

Houses and homes

Around the world, people live in all kinds of different homes. They build them out of materials they find nearby. Some houses are made of bricks or stone. Others are made of wood, mud, or reeds.

Some people are nomads. This means that they move from place to place. These nomads in Mongolia live in round tents called "yurts."

People who live near rivers and marshes often build their houses on stilts, like this house in Indonesia. It is raised high above the ground, safe from flooding.

230

n North Africa, some houses are built of mud, with thick walls and small windows to keep out the sun.

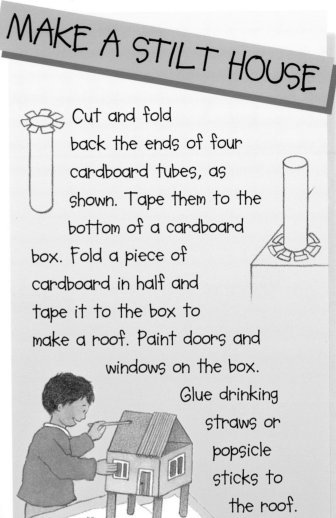

Cut and fold back the ends of four cardboard tubes, as shown. Tape them to the bottom of a cardboard box. Fold a piece of cardboard in half and tape it to the box to make a roof. Paint doors and windows on the box. Glue drinking straws or popsicle sticks to the roof.

Apartment buildings, like this one in Africa, are built in cities where there is not much room to build. They let more people live in a smaller space.

This American house was built from bricks and wood. Both materials were easy to buy nearby.

Jobs people do

People do all kinds of different jobs. They work to earn money to buy the things they need. Most people start working when they leave high school or college.

Teachers work in schools and colleges. They teach their students how to read and write, and many other things that they need to know. Some teachers teach all kinds of subjects. Others teach just one subject.

Health workers teach people how they can stay strong and healthy. This woman is holding a clinic for mothers and their babies.

Construction workers work in teams to build new homes, offices, and other buildings. This man is a bricklayer. He is carrying the bricks with which he builds walls.

Many people work with machines that make things. This man is in charge of a machine that makes bread, slices it, and wraps it in plastic.

Industry

Industries produce things that people need. Many industries make things, such as cars or buildings. Others produce the raw materials needed to make things, such as metal or oil.

The automobile industry produces cars. Billions of cars are made in factories every year. Most of them are put together on conveyor belts by robots.

Oil is needed to run machinery. There is oil buried under the ocean, so oil rigs are built on high platforms in the water. They drill deep into the seabed and pump the oil up to the surface.

Robot arm

Anchors hold oil platform in place

Helicopter landing pad

Crane

Drill

Many people work together to put up buildings. They use giant machines, like this crane, to lift huge pieces of buildings into place.

Scientists study chemicals. They figure out how to make medicines, plastics, and many other things that people use every day.

Land and sea

Farmers and fishermen work hard to produce all the food that we eat. Some farmers grow crops, such as cereals, fruit, or vegetables. Others keep animals. Fishermen catch fish and send them to markets to be sold.

There are thousands of sheep on a big Australian sheep farm like this. Sheep farmers rear sheep to sell for meat. They also shear the sheep—clip off their fleece— and sell the wool.

236

A lot of rice is grown in Asia (below). Rice needs a lot of water, so it is grown in flooded fields called paddy fields. The rice is often harvested by hand, using sharp tools called sickles.

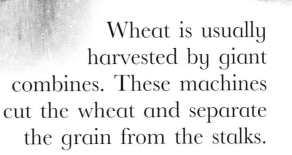

Wheat is usually harvested by giant combines. These machines cut the wheat and separate the grain from the stalks.

Most fish are caught in huge nets pulled behind big boats called trawlers. On board, the fishermen pack the fish in ice to keep them fresh.

Food

Around the world, people cook and eat many different kinds of food. Some countries have their own special meals. For example, Italy is famous for delicious pasta dishes and India for spicy curries.

In Asia, kabobs are served with a peanut sauce called satay.

France is famous for its fine cooking. Below is a French salad made with tuna, potatoes, egg, and olives. Next to it is a loaf of French bread.

Sushi is a traditional Japanese dish. Small pieces of raw fish are arranged on rice.

Paella is made in Spain. Rice is cooked with vegetables and chicken or fish. The rice is colored with a yellow spice called saffron.

Chow mein is a Chinese dish. Egg noodles are fried in a big pan with chopped vegetables and meat or seafood.

Hamburgers come from the United States. They are often served with lettuce and tomatoes in a big, soft bun.

FUNNY FACE PIZZA

Ask an adult to slice some cheese, tomatoes, mushrooms, and peppers. Spread tomato sauce on a pizza base. Arrange the vegetables on the base in funny face shapes. Cook in a 375° oven for 10–12 minutes.

Clothes

People wear clothes to keep themselves warm and comfortable. They put different clothes on depending on what they are doing, or whether it is hot or cold.

Many children like to wear comfortable clothes that they can run around in.

People who live in cold places wear many layers of clothing to keep themselves warm. All their outdoor clothes and shoes are waterproof, to keep out rain and snow.

In India, the traditional dress for women is called a sari. It is made of a long piece of material draped around the body.

In hot countries, people often wear loose robes to keep cool. These Masai women are wearing large beaded collars for a celebration.

These athletes are wearing special sportswear. Their clothes fit tightly and are made of stretchy material in which it is easy to move. Other athletes sometimes wear pads and helmets that protect them from injuries.

Arts and crafts

Around the world, people make all kinds of decorative things. Some people paint pictures. Others shape pots, make jewelry, or weave rugs. These skills, called crafts, are often handed down from parent to child.

The Navajo people make sand pictures on the ground for special ceremonies. The patterns are made from grains of different colored sand. Some of the pictures include magic signs.

Many countries make fine china. The same patterns are often used again and again

Some African people make masks out of clay, wood, or metal, to wear at special ceremonies.

These brightly patterned pieces of fabric come from Ghana, in West Africa. They are woven from cotton dyed in many different colors.

In Turkmenistan, in Asia, women weave yarn into colorful, patterned carpets. The country is famous for its carpets. They have been made the same way for thousands of years.

MAKE A RUG

Fold a piece of construction paper in half. Cut slits in it, as shown. Open the paper and tape strips of colored paper to one edge. Weave the strips in and out of the slits until you get to the other edge. Tape the strips in place. Weave enough strips to make a colorful rug.

Festivals

Festivals are large celebrations with music, dancing, colorful costumes, and entertainment. Most festivals mark special days or events. Many are linked to a religion, while others may just celebrate the changing seasons.

Chinese people celebrate their New Year with a festival. Huge, brightly colored dragons lead processions through the streets. People carry lanterns and set off fireworks.

In Sweden, people decorate a pole and dance around it to celebrate Midsummer's Eve.

During the
Japanese festival Hinamatsuri,
people float paper flowers or dolls
down a river to make their
problems go away.

DECORATE SOME EGGS

Ask an adult to
make small holes in the ends
of some eggs. Blow out the
insides, and rinse and dry
the eggs. To
paper an egg,
paste small
squares of paper all over
it. To paint an egg,
paint patterns on one
half first. Let the
paint dry, then paint
the other half.

On Halloween, on
October 31, people in
the United States make
spooky jack-o'-lanterns
to scare away evil spirits.

Many Christians celebrate
Easter by giving each
other decorated eggs, or
eggs made from chocolate.

Music and dance

All around the world, people love music and dancing. They play hundreds of different musical instruments and enjoy many different kinds of music. Most countries have their own traditional music and dances.

Ballet is a graceful way of dancing that is based on set movements. Ballet dancers train for many years to learn to perform the different steps.

This Indonesian percussion orchestra is called a gamelan. The musicians play xylophones, chimes, gongs, and drums.

Music and dance play an important part in celebrations. At the festival of Esala Perahera in Sri Lanka, drummers and dancers parade next to elephants in decorative costumes.

MAKE MARACAS

Pour rice or dried beans into a plastic cup. Stand another plastic cup upside down on top of it and tape the two edges together. Make two, decorate them, then try shaking them!

The flute and the recorder are both wind instruments. This means you blow into them. You cover the holes with your fingers to make different notes.

Entertainment

There are many ways to relax and enjoy yourself. You could go out to see a play or a movie, or visit an amusement park. Sometimes you may prefer to read a book or play computer games.

At shadow puppet shows in Java, the audience sits on both sides of a screen. Half of them watch the puppets, while the other half watch the shadows on the screen.

Amusement parks are very popular for exciting days out. There are many attractions, like the scary roller coaster.

Towns and cities often hold big firework displays to celebrate a special occasion or time of the year. People watch as fireworks shoot into the night sky and explode in fantastic patterns and colors.

If you wear this headset and glove, you will be whisked into another world! They are connected to a computer that creates pictures and sounds. This is called virtual reality.

251

Sports and hobbies

Many people love sports and games. They are fun to watch and play, and they can help keep you fit, too. Many people also have hobbies. These are things they like to do in their spare time.

Ice hockey is a fast, tough game played on an ice rink. The players wear ice skates and helmets, and use special sticks to slide a flat disk, called a puck, into the goal.

In a basketball game there are two teams. They have to throw the ball into the basket to score points.

Soccer is one of the most popular sports and is played all over the world. Most countries have a national team that plays against other countries.

Chess is a board game for two players. It is like a battle. The players take turns moving and trying to capture each other's chess pieces.

Many children have a personal computer at home. They can use it for doing their homework, exploring the Internet, or playing all sorts of different games.

Trains, Boats, and Planes

Cars

Cars come in many shapes and sizes. People use them to go to work or to school, to go shopping, or to go on vacation. Most cars have engines that run on gas. They usually have four wheels.

A superstretch limousine is a very, very long car. This one is the longest car in the world. It has 26 wheels and its own luxury swimming pool in the back.

This sports utility vehicle was designed for driving across rough ground. Its powerful engine drives all four wheels, instead of just the two in the back. This is called four-wheel drive.

Sports cars are designed for speed. They have large engines and a smooth, flat shape that helps them go fast. Most sports cars only have seats for two people.

Designers have been trying to invent a car that doesn't need gas. This car has a large solar panel. It uses rays from the Sun to make energy to drive the car.

Racing vehicles

Some cars and motorcycles are built especially for racing. They are designed to go as fast as possible. Racing vehicles speed around special circuits or tracks. They are not driven on ordinary roads.

Formula One race cars have enormously powerful engines and can drive at speeds of more than 120 miles an hour. Drivers compete with each other on racetracks all over the world.

This race car has a special "wing" at the back. It does not work like an airplane's wings. Instead of lifting the car, it keeps it on the track when it is going fast.

These trail bikes are specially designed for off-road racing. They can scramble over muddy or rocky ground, and up and down steep hills.

Trucks and tractors

Trucks and tractors are working machines. They are used to pull heavy loads, and often deliver goods across great distances. They need to be strong and sturdy and have very powerful engines.

A semitrailer pulls heavy loads on long journeys. The truck is made up of two sections so that it can bend in the middle. This helps it go around tight corners.

Tractors are used to pull and operate many different farm machines. A tractor's giant back wheels have big, ridged tires. These stop the tractor from slipping on muddy ground.

The truck's load is carried in the trailer.

A tanker is a type of truck that carries liquids, such as gas or milk, in cylinder-shaped tanks. Some tankers have several tanks linked together.

The trailer is joined to the "fifth wheel."

The tractor unit has a sleeping cabin, where the driver sleeps on long journeys.

The tractor unit pulls the trailer. Its fuel is stored in huge tanks.

Diggers and dumper

Most of the heavy work on construction sites is done by machines. There are different machines for different jobs. Some dig holes, some lift building materials, and others dump huge loads of rubble.

A dump truck carries dirt and rocks, then unloads them wherever they are needed. There are sliding arms called pistons underneath the back of the truck. These tip it up so that it can dump its load.

This backhoe is used to dig holes and move heavy loads. It has a wide bucket at the front for moving rubble. At the back it has a rounded bucket attached to a strong arm. This digs holes and scoops dirt and rocks into trucks.

MAKE A PULLEY

With an adult, unbend a wire coathanger and push a spool onto it. Hang the hanger on a hook. Tie string to a bucket handle and thread the string over the spool. Pull the other end of the string to lift the bucket.

A mobile crane has a long arm called a boom. This can reach up high to pick up heavy loads. The loads are lifted by strong wire cables that run along the boom and around pulleys at the base of the crane.

269

Trains

Trains run on rails. They are made of cars pulled by engines. Passenger trains carry people, and freight trains transport goods. The first trains were powered by steam, but most modern trains run on electricity or a fuel called diesel.

The Mallard recorded the fastest speed ever for a steam train. It reached a speed of 126 miles an hour.

The fastest passenger train in the world is the French TGV. TGV stands for "high speed train" in French. It travels at more than 185 miles an hour. In this picture, you can see the insides of the train. It runs on electricity from the wires above.

Glue two boxes together to make an engine. Make the chimney and buffers out of cardboard tubes. Use more boxes for cars, and paper plates for wheels.

In the United States, powerful diesel engines pull freight trains across the country from coast to coast. The engines are strong enough to pull the cars and their heavy cargo up mountains.

Tunnels and bridges

Tunnels and bridges make journeys shorter and easier. Bridges take roads and railroads over obstacles, such as rivers and highways. Tunnels are cut through mountains and under rivers and seas.

To build tunnels, people cut through the rock with giant tunneling machines, or blast huge holes using explosives.

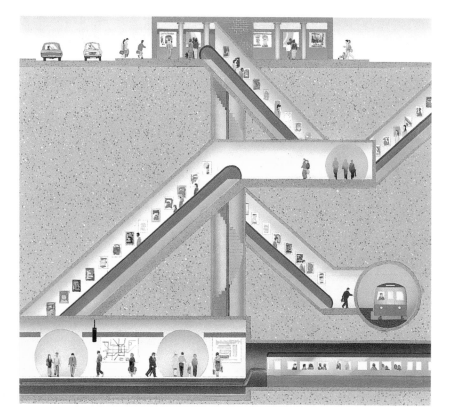

Subways are built in tunnels that run underneath big cities. Here you can see that different lines, going in different directions, are built at different depths.

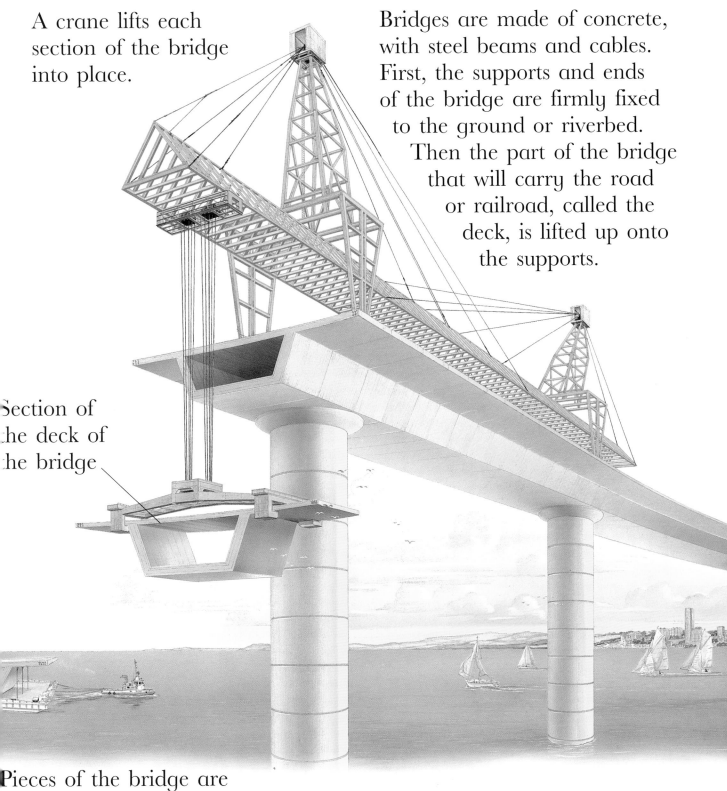

A crane lifts each section of the bridge into place.

Bridges are made of concrete, with steel beams and cables. First, the supports and ends of the bridge are firmly fixed to the ground or riverbed. Then the part of the bridge that will carry the road or railroad, called the deck, is lifted up onto the supports.

Section of the deck of the bridge

Pieces of the bridge are brought to the site by boat.

Ships and boats

People have built many different ships and boats to carry them along rivers and across oceans. They might want to explore new lands, or just go on vacation. Some ships carry passengers very fast; others go more slowly.

Ships like this galleon were used for early sea voyages. They were driven along by the wind, so their journeys often took months.

This is one of the first steam-powered boats. It burned wood or coal to make steam to turn a paddle wheel at the back of the boat.

274

This modern ferry, called a catamaran, has two hulls. This makes it very steady in the water. It can speed along without tilting from side to side.

Hull

A slow cruise liner is like a floating hotel. There are all sorts of things to do on board. The liner carries passengers on long sea journeys, calling at many different ports. The liner's engines drive huge propellers that go around under the water.

MAKE A CATAMARAN

Ask an adult to cut a plastic bottle in half lengthwise, to make two hulls. Stick thin strips of balsa wood across the hulls with waterproof tape to hold them together. Fill a big bowl with water and try floating your catamaran in it.

Submarines

Submarines can travel beneath the ocean for many weeks without coming up to the surface. Many submarines are underwater warships that carry missiles and other dangerous weapons. Others are used to explore the depths of the sea.

1

2

The first submarine used in warfare could only carry one person. He had to turn the propeller, steer the submarine to an enemy ship, and hook a bomb to its hull. This did not work, so the submarine was only used once.

Small underwater vessels are called submersibles. They dive deep in the ocean to repair underwater cables and pipelines, or to carry out research. This one has robotic arms that can pick up and move things.

1 Propeller
2 Rudder
3 Hydroplane
4 Periscope

Large submarines have diesel or nuclear-powered engines that turn a propeller to move them through the water. The rudder steers and the hydroplane controls how deep a submarine goes. The captain uses a tube called a periscope to see what is above the surface of the water.

In the air

There are many kinds of flying machines. They all fly in different ways. Some can fly very fast, while others can do tricks in the air, such as turning upside down.

A blimp is filled with a very light gas called helium. It is not like a hot-air balloon, because it has an engine. This means that it can be steered and controlled easily. Blimps are mainly used for advertising or for taking photographs from the air.

Airliners are a fast way to travel. They carry passengers all around the world. This passenger jet can hold about 250 people.

MAKE A GYROCOPTER

Cut a piece of paper 6 inches long and 1½ inches wide. Cut a slit 3 inches long down the middle. Fold the two flaps down. Attach a paper clip to the bottom of the paper. Drop the gyrocopter from a height. It will spin to the ground.

A jump jet is a fighter plane that can take off and land vertically. It rises straight off the ground without needing a runway. It can also turn very sharply and hover in midair like a helicopter.

A helicopter has rotor blades on its roof and its tail. They make it fly. It can move back and forth and sideways, or hover in the air.

Traveling by air

Airliners are large airplanes with powerful jet engines. They can travel at speeds of more than 600 miles an hour. Airliners carry passengers great distances between countries very quickly.

A modern jumbo jet carries over 400 passengers. The pilot and copilot who fly the plane sit in the flight deck.

Fuel is stored inside the wings

Seats where the passengers sit

Jet engine

Flight deck

The tail fin helps keep the plane steady

For the wing, cut out a piece of stiff paper 9½ inches by 5 inches. Tape the long sides together. Cut two slits in the taped edge and fold back two flaps. Cut out another piece of paper 8 inches by 1½ inches for the tail. Fold the middle so it sticks up. Cut off ½ inch of the flat pieces on each side of the tail, then make flaps in the flat edges. Tape the wing and tail to a drinking straw as shown to make your plane. Attach paper clips to the front of the straw to make it heavier. Now try flying the plane.

These flaps make the plane go up or down

Flaps called ailerons make the plane turn left or right

When you have made your glider, try moving the flaps up and down, and the back of the tail from side to side. How does it affect the flight?

Rescue vehicles

When there is an accident or a fire, special vehicles rush to the scene. They are specially equipped to rescue people and save buildings. The police, the fire department, and the ambulance service are the main emergency services.

The police use fast cars or bikes with sirens and flashing lights to reach the scene quickly.

Each emergency service does a different job. Ambulances rush injured people to the hospital for treatment. They have beds and medical equipment inside them. Trained staff lift people into the ambulance on stretchers and look after them until they arrive at the hospital.

Fire engines have extendable
ladders on turntables
that reach high
up buildings.

Fire fighters point
their powerful hoses
at the flames to
put out the fire.

124

What is science?

Science is the way we find out about the world around us. Scientists look at everything carefully so that they can understand why things happen the way they do. They learn new things all the time.

Sometimes scientists use special tools, such as this magnifying glass, to help them study things close up.

Scientists try to answer questions about everyday things, such as "What are bubbles?" and "How do we hear different sounds?"

Scientists ask questions about the world and guess what the answers might be. Then they do experiments to test whether their theories are right.

"How does an airplane fly?" You can be a scientist too, by asking questions about things you see around you.

Often, you can find out what you want to know from books or the Internet. Or you could try doing simple experiments of your own at home to test your ideas.

What is it made of?

The things around you are not all made out of the same material. They are made from different materials, depending on what they are for. Materials can be soft, hard, heavy, light, rough, or smooth.

Do you know what your toys are made of? Soft things might be made of yarn or fabric. Smooth things can be made of metal, plastic, or glass.

Plastic

Fabric

Metal

Imitation fur

Paper

Water

Ice

Steam

Everything is either a liquid, a solid, or a gas. Liquids are runny. Solids have a fixed shape. Gases spread out to fill the space they are in. Some materials can change from one thing to another. Water is liquid, but when it freezes it turns into solid ice. If water boils, some of it becomes a gas called steam.

HOMEMADE POPSICLES

Pour your favorite fruit juice into a popsicle mold and put it in the freezer. When the popsicles are frozen, hold the mold under a warm tap for a few seconds, then gently slip them out of the mold.

Wood

Glass

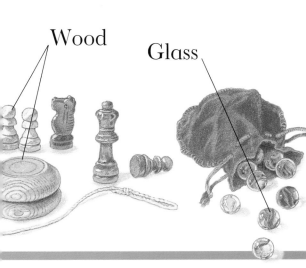

The air around us

Air is all around you, but you cannot see it, smell it, or taste it. Air has no shape and spreads out to fill every space. It is a mixture of different gases. One of these is oxygen, which all animals need to breathe in order to live.

Hot-air balloons have hot air inside them. The hot air is lighter than the cold air around the balloon, so the balloon rises into the sky and flies.

Wind is moving air. People use the wind's power to fill the sails of boats and push them along.

Cut slits in a square of construction paper, taking care not to cut all the way to the center. Fold the corners into the middle and push a pin through them. Thread on a bead. Push the pin through a plastic drinking straw, a bead, and a piece of cork. Blow on the pinwheel to make it spin.

Hang gliders launch themselves into the air from high places. Then they glide through the sky on currents of warm air called thermals. Thermals rise up into the sky from the land.

A flying lemur cannot really fly. As it jumps from tree to tree, it spreads out flaps of skin between its arms and legs. These help it to glide through the air.

291

Hot and cold

Heat never stays in one place. It moves around all the time, spreading out from warm places to colder ones. This is why hot things cool down and cold things warm up.

Loose clothes let air flow around the body. People in hot countries often wear loose clothing to keep cool.

A radiator is filled with hot water. The heat spreads from the radiator to warm up the rest of the room.

It is very
warm inside
a greenhouse.
The glass walls let
the Sun's rays pass
through them, but they
do not let the heat escape.

The water in this metal
saucepan is being heated on a
stove. The heat passes from the
stove to the saucepan and then
to the water. Metal is used to
make saucepans because heat
travels through it very easily.

Water

Water is an extraordinary liquid. Sometimes it dries up and just disappears—think of a puddle on a sunny day. At other times, drops of water seem to appear from nowhere. Where do they come from?

Ask an adult to boil a cup of water in a saucepan for five minutes. Let the water cool, then pour it back into the cup. There is less water now. When water boils, some of it turns into an invisible gas called water vapor. This is called evaporation.

When you take a hot shower, some of the water evaporates. As the water vapor cools down, tiny droplets of water form again in the air and you see steam.

Insects called water striders can walk across water without sinking. This is because the surface of water is like a thin, stretchy skin, strong enough to support the weight of an insect. This is called surface tension.

BUBBLE TROUBLE

Gently touch a drop of water with a soapy straw. The drop of water will spread out. The soap on the straw weakens the water's skin, or surface tension. It is no longer able to hold the drop in its rounded shape.

When water vapor hits a cold surface, such as a mirror, it cools down suddenly and turns back into small drops of water again. This is called condensation.

Floating

Some things can float in water. Objects are pulled down by their weight, but the water pushes them up. If something is light for its size, the water will be able to hold it up and it will float.

Giant icebergs float in the ocean because ice is lighter than water. They can even support the weight of polar bears.

Water wings keep you from sinking when you are learning to swim. This is because they are full of air.

Air is much lighter than water, so it helps you float and keeps you safe.

MAKE A CLAY BOAT

Drop a lump of modeling clay into a bowl of water, and it will sink. Make a boat from another ball of modeling clay the same size, and it will float. The boat has a much larger surface than the ball of clay. This makes it lighter for its size, so it can float.

Whether or not an object floats depends on its shape and what it is made out of. Objects made of metal or glass don't usually float. Wooden objects float well. If an object is filled with air it will float better.

Light

Without light, we
would not be able
to see. Most of
our light comes
from the Sun.
It travels through
space very fast.
Light is made by
hot or burning things.
Fires, light bulbs, and
fireworks all make light.

The Moon cannot
make its own light.
The moonlight we see
is really light from the
Sun bouncing off the
Moon. The Sun gives
off light all the time,
because it is a giant
ball of burning gases.

MAKE SHADOW PUPPETS

Turn off the light in your room and ask a friend to shine a flashlight on the wall beside you. Put your hands between the flashlight and the wall, then hold them in these different positions to make animal shadows on the wall. Take turns holding the flashlight and making animal shadows.

Dog

Giraffe

Bird

When light hits a smooth, shiny surface, like this puddle, it bounces back again and you see a reflection.

Light only travels in straight lines. It will not bend around things. If you block the Sun's light, you make a shadow. At noon, the Sun is high in the sky and your shadow is short.

Your shadow is always longer in the early morning or late afternoon.

Colors

Sunlight looks colorless, but in fact it is a mixture of different colors. You see all these colors in a rainbow, as the raindrops split the sunlight.

On a sunny day, you can make a rainbow with a hose. Stand with your back to the Sun and make a fine spray. You will see red, orange, yellow, green, blue, indigo, and violet

Blue, red, and yellow are called primary colors. By mixing them together, you can make most other colors except white.

ROSE-COLORED GLASSES

Draw glasses frames on a piece of cardboard. Copy a pair of glasses you have at home to make them the right size. Cut the glasses out and fold back the arms. Tape pink cellophane candy wrappers across the eyeholes on the back of the frames. Color and decorate the frames.

Many animals use color to hide from other animals that might eat them. This leaf insect is the same color as the leaves it sits on, so it is hard to see.

The bright patterns on a butterfly's wings help it attract a mate. The blue eyespots also trick hungry hunters into thinking it is not a butterfly.

Time

The clocks and watches we use to tell time are very accurate. Long ago people could only count the days and nights to measure the passing of time. Later, they invented simple clocks using water or sand to tell the time.

The first number on this watch is the hour. The second number is the minutes. The smaller numbers show the seconds. There are 60 seconds in a minute and 60 minutes in an hour.

An egg timer works like a sandglass. The sand runs from one half of the timer to the other in exactly the time it takes to boil an egg. To start the timer, you turn it upside down to make the sand run into the empty half.

MAKE A WATER CLOCK

Ask an adult to
make a small hole in the bottom of
a plastic pot. Tape a string handle
to it. Pin it under an old table.
Stand an empty, clear plastic pot
under the hanging pot. Pour water
into the top pot. After each minute,
mark the water level on the bottom
pot. You can now use the marks as
a clock to
measure
minutes.

A clock face has 12 numbers on it, one for each hour. The short hand points to the hours. It moves around the clock twice a day because there are 24 hours in a day. The long hand shows how many minutes past the hour it is. It moves around the clock once an hour, or every 60 minutes.

Sounds

There are sounds around us all the time—voices, music, traffic. Every sound you hear is made by something vibrating. This means that it is moving back and forth very quickly.

Sound can also travel through solid things. This boy can hear the girl banging the saucepan through the tabletop.

Sound moves through the air in waves. When someone speaks to you, they make vibrations in the air. The sound waves travel through the air to you. Your ears pick up the vibrations, and you hear sounds.

In a bottle organ, each bottle makes a different sound when you strike it. The more water there is in a bottle, the higher the sound it makes.

SEEING SOUNDS

You cannot see sound waves, but you can see their effects. Stretch some tinfoil tightly over a bowl. Fasten it with a rubber band to make a drum. Put some grains of uncooked rice on the drum, then bang a metal tray next to it. The sound waves will make the rice jump.

Sound travels four times faster through water than it does through air. It also travels much farther. Seals can hear each other underwater even when they are very far apart.

Movement

Movement uses energy, so all moving objects have to get the energy they need from somewhere. There are many different ways to do this.

Inside a vehicle, there is an engine that burns fuel, such as diesel oil or gas. When this fuel is burned, it releases energy that the vehicle uses to move.

Surfers use the ocean's energy to move. They wait for a big wave, then surf along it as it breaks. They are carried forward by the movement of the water

You get energy from the food you eat. When you ride a bike, you use energy stored inside your body. You need to eat regularly so that you do not run out of energy.

Like all animals, these kangaroos get their energy from the food they eat.

You use your own energy to start a toboggan by giving it a push. When it is going downhill, the toboggan has enough energy to keep moving by itself.

Weight

The Earth is like a big magnet. It pulls things toward it. This pull is called gravity. It keeps you on the ground and makes the balls you throw into the air come back down again. Gravity also affects how much things weigh.

The pull of gravity makes apples fall from a tree to the ground when they have grown big and heavy.

When you weigh yourself or an apple, the scales are actually measuring the pull of Earth's gravity on the apple and you. The greater the pull of gravity on an object, the more it weighs.

A seesaw is like
a balancing scale.
It balances when the
weight at each end is
the same. This seesaw will
not move because it weighs
more at one end than the
other. One of the children
is getting off to make
the weight even.

When the
children at
both ends of
the seesaw weigh
about the same,
it is easy to make
the seesaw go
up and down.

A balancing toy swings from side
to side, but it does not fall over
because both sides of it weigh the
same. It stands upright on its
balancing point.

Magnets

Magnets can pull—or attract—things toward them. Materials that are attracted to magnets are called magnetic. Most metals are magnetic, but paper, plastic, and wood are not.

Nonmagnetic objects

Magnetic objects

Collect objects from around your home and test them with a magnet to see which materials are magnetic.

North pole

South pole

North pole

The ends of a magnet are called its north and south poles. The two poles are different. The north pole of one magnet attracts the south pole of another magnet. Two north poles or two south poles push each other apart.

South pole

Junkyards use giant magnets attached to cranes to lift scrap metal. The magnets are so strong that they can even lift cars!

Electricity

Electricity can be used to make heat and light and to power all kinds of machinery. It runs through all the wires in your home. Small amounts can also be stored in batteries.

This toaster runs on electricity. You can plug machines into the sockets around your home to make them work. Be careful when using electricity—you could get a dangerous electric shock.

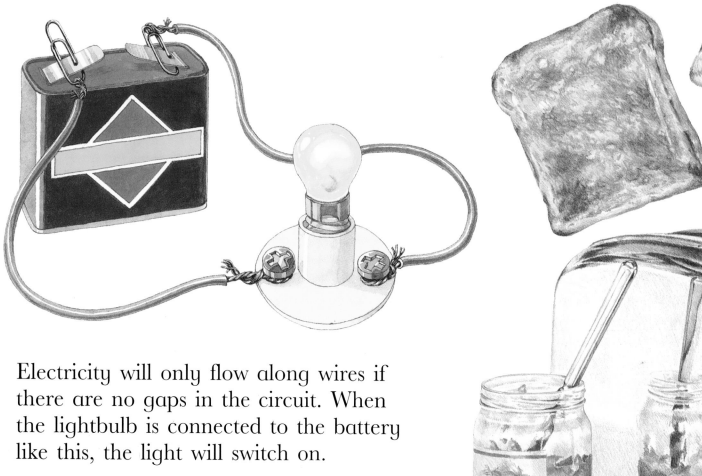

Electricity will only flow along wires if there are no gaps in the circuit. When the lightbulb is connected to the battery like this, the light will switch on.

MAKE A SIMPLE CIRCUIT

Ask an adult to help.

Screw a small bulb into a bulb holder.

Strip ½ inch of plastic from each end of two pieces of electrical wire. Attach one end of each piece to a screw on the bulb holder.

Attach paper clips to the other ends and clip them to the battery terminals.

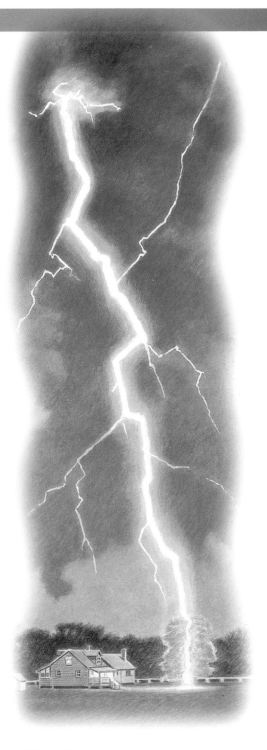

The lightning you see during a thunderstorm is electricity, but it is not the same as the electricity you use at home. Lightning is called static electricity.

313

Everyday science

Science and new inventions have become a part of our daily lives. Our homes are full of machines that help us do things more easily. Many things are also made by machines.

A radio cassette player is plugged into an electric socket

Look around your room. Many of your things are made of plastic and other manufactured materials. How many different machines are there in your room? Are they plugged in, or do they run on batteries?

This digital alarm clock runs on batteries

You may use a computer for your homework, or to play games

Sneakers are designed on a computer and made by machine.

Index

If you want to read about a subject, use this index to find out where it is in the book. It is in alphabetical order.

a

b

c

Acknowledgments

The publishers would like to thank the following artists for their contributions to this book:

Hemesh Alles, Marion Appleton, Mike Atkinson, Craig Austin, Julian Baker, Julie Banyard, John Barber, Andrew Beckett, Tim Beer, Richard Bonson, Derick Bown, Maggie Brand, Derek Brazell, Peter Bull, John Butler, Martin Camm, Jim Channel, Robin Carter, Adrian Chesterman, Dan Cole, Jeanne Colville, Tom Connell, Joanne Cowne, Peter Dennis, Sandra Doyle, Richard Draper, Brin Edwards, Colin Emberson, Diane Fawcett, James Field, Michael Fisher, Chris Fobey, Chris Forsey, Andrew French, Terence J. Gabbey, Peter Goodfellow, Ruby Green, Ray Grinaway, Terry Hadler, Nick Hawken, Tim Hayward, Karen Hiscock, David Holmes, Steve Holmes, Adam Hook, Christian Hook, Liza Horstman, Biz Hull, Mark Iley, Ian Jackson, Rob Jobson, Kevin Jones, Pete Kelly, Roger Kent, Tony Kenyon, David Kerney, Deborah Kindred, Steve Kirk, Mike Lacey, Stuart Lafford, Terence Lambert, Ruth Lindsay, Bernard Long, Chris Lyon, Kevin Maddison, Alan Male, Adam Marshall, Josephine Martin, David McAllister, Doreen McGuiness, Eva Melhuish, Steve Noon, Chris Orr, Nicki Palin, Darren Pattenden, Bruce Pearson, Liz Pepperell, Jane Pickering, Maurice Pledger, John Potter, Nigel Quigley, Sebastian Quigley, Elizabeth Rice, John Ridyard, John Rignall, Gordon Riley, Bernard Robinson, Eric Robinson, Eric Robson, Mike Roffe, David Russell, Mike Saunders, John Scory, Stephen Seymour, Rob Shone, Guy Smith, Clive Spong, Mark Stewart, Charlotte Stowell, Lucy Su, Treve Tamblin, Myke Taylor, Ian Thompson, Jean Paul Tibbles, Chris Turnball, Richard Ward, Ross Watton, Phil Weare, Rhian West James, Steve Weston, Lynne Willey, Ann Winterbotham, David Woods, Dan Wright, David Wright

Every effort has been made to credit the artists whose work appears in this book. The publishers apologize for any inadvertent omissions. We will be pleased to amend the acknowledgments in any future editions.